My Brother's Secret

Also by Maggie Hartley

Tiny Prisoners
Too Scared to Cry
The Little Ghost Girl
A Family for Christmas
Too Young to be a Mum
Who Will Love Me Now?
The Girl No One Wanted
Battered, Broken, Healed
Is it My Fault, Mummy?
Sold to be a Wife
Denied a Mummy
A Desperate Cry for Help
Daddy's Little Soldier
Please, Don't Take My Sisters
Not to Blame
Exploited
Groomed to be a Bride
The Lost Boy
A Sister's Shame
Behind Closed Doors
Please Give My Baby Back
Where's My Mummy?
Nobody Loves Me
Please Don't Take Mummy Away
Will You Help Me?
A Sister for Christmas
Please Help My Mummy
Don't Leave Me Here

My Brother's Secret

CAN THREE NEGLECTED BROTHERS STAY TOGETHER, OR WILL THEY BE TORN APART?

MAGGIE HARTLEY

WITH
HEATHER BISHOP

SEVEN DIALS

First published in Great Britain in 2026 by Seven Dials,
an imprint of The Orion Publishing Group Ltd
Carmelite House, 50 Victoria Embankment
London EC4Y 0DZ

An Hachette UK Company

The authorised representative in the EEA is Hachette Ireland,
8 Castlecourt Centre, Dublin 15, D15 XTP3, Ireland
(email: info@hbgi.ie)

1 3 5 7 9 10 8 6 4 2

Copyright © Maggie Hartley Limited 2026

The moral right of Maggie Hartley to be identified as
the author of this work has been asserted in accordance
with the Copyright, Designs and Patents Act of 1988.

All rights reserved. No part of this publication may be
reproduced, stored in a retrieval system, or transmitted
in any form or by any means, electronic, mechanical,
photocopying, recording, or otherwise, without the
prior permission of both the copyright owner and the
above publisher of this book.

A CIP catalogue record for this book is
available from the British Library.

**Please be aware that this book includes discussions of a
range of sensitive subjects, including abuse.**

ISBN (Mass Market Paperback) 9781399638548
ISBN (Ebook) 9781399638555
ISBN (Audio) 9781399638562

Typeset by Born Group
Printed and bound in Great Britain by Clays Ltd, Elcograf S.p.A.

www.orionbooks.co.uk

Dedication

This book is dedicated to Amber, Cooper, Keegan and Billy, and all the children who have passed through my home. It's been a privilege to have cared for you and to have been able to share your stories. And to the children who live with me now. Thank you for your determination, strength and joy, and for sharing your lives with me.

Contents

	A Message from Maggie	xi
ONE	*Expectations*	1
TWO	*A Proposition*	11
THREE	*New Arrivals*	21
FOUR	*Pushing the Boundaries*	33
FIVE	*Reconnecting*	47
SIX	*Whirlwind of Destruction*	59
SEVEN	*Confessions*	71
EIGHT	*Introductions*	81
NINE	*One In, One Out*	97
TEN	*Off the Rails*	111
ELEVEN	*Hidden Dangers*	123
TWELVE	*Denial*	133

THIRTEEN	*The Wrong Brother*	143
FOURTEEN	*Questions*	157
FIFTEEN	*Shockwaves*	165
SIXTEEN	*Fallout*	175
SEVENTEEN	*Reunions*	185
EIGHTEEN	*Rough Justice*	197
NINETEEN	*Second Chances*	209
	Acknowledgements	223

A Message from Maggie

I wanted to write this book to give people an honest account about what it's like to be a foster carer. To talk about some of the challenges that I face on a day-to-day basis and some of the children that I've helped. This book deals with the topic of fostering a sibling group. It's not uncommon to foster sibling groups but it had been a while since I'd fostered three children from the same family.

My main concern throughout all this is to protect the children that have been in my care. For this reason, all names and identifying details have been changed, including my own, and no locations have been included. But I can assure you that all my stories are based on real-life cases told from my own experiences.

Being a foster carer is a privilege and I couldn't imagine doing anything else. My house is never quiet but I wouldn't have it any other way. I hope that perhaps my stories inspire other people to consider fostering, as new carers are always desperately needed. In fact, there's currently a recruitment crisis facing the fostering community – across the UK, there's currently a shortfall of 6,000 foster carers and the UK is experiencing the lowest number of foster carers in a decade.[*] It comes at the same time as there are approximately 107,000 children in care across the UK.[†] Foster carers are needed more than ever so please do look into it, if it's something that you or someone you know has ever considered.

---

[*] The Fostering Network. 'Crisis in foster care continues as new figures show major shortfall in carers'. Available at: https://www.thefosteringnetwork.org.uk/news/crisis-in-foster-care-continues-as-new-figures-show-major-shortfall-in-carers/ (accessed 11 November 2025).

[†] NSPCC. 'Children in care: statistics briefing'. Available at: https://learning.nspcc.org.uk/research-resources/statistics-briefings/children-in-care (accessed 10 December 2025).

ONE

Expectations

The kitchen was filled with the sound of chatter and laughter, just as I liked it.

'Nana, Amber says you've got cake for pudding,' my four-year-old granddaughter Edie told me with a cheeky smile. 'A chocolate cake.'

'Did she now?' I teased. 'That depends if everyone has eaten their pasta.'

'I have!' yelled four-year-old Amber.

'Me have too,' Edie quickly added.

She looked over at her mum, Louisa, whose plate was barely touched.

'But Mummy hasn't,' she said.

'Well, there'll be no cake for Mummy then,' I laughed.

'Sorry,' sighed Louisa, pushing her plate away. 'It was lovely, it really was. I just had a big lunch and I'm still pretty full.'

'Don't worry, lovey,' I said, putting my hand on hers. 'I'm only teasing you. I'm not going to force you to finish it.'

I turned to the girls.

'Why don't you two go and play while I clear up then I'll get the cake ready?'

'OK, Nana,' nodded Edie. 'Come on, Amber.'

As they ran off to play in the front room, I smiled.

'Edie's so grown up these days,' I sighed.

'I know,' nodded Louisa. 'I can't believe she'll be off to school in a few months.'

I'd started fostering Louisa when she was thirteen, after her parents had been tragically killed in a car crash. We had our ups and downs and she'd spent months recovering physically from the crash as well as dealing with the crippling pain of her grief. It had taken Louisa many years to adjust to a life without her beloved parents. When she left the care system at eighteen, she chose to carry on living with me. I saw her as a daughter and I couldn't have loved her any more if she was my biological child.

I was so proud of Louisa and it was lovely to see her now living her own life, happily married to Charlie and being a brilliant mum to Edie.

Edie called me Nana and she was, to all intents and purposes, my granddaughter and there was no doubt she had me well and truly wrapped around her little finger.

'How's Amber getting on?' Louisa asked me.

'She was very unsettled at first but she's slowly getting there,' I nodded.

Four-year-old Amber had come to live with me two months ago. Her mum, Petra, had fallen into a bad relationship and become addicted to heroin. Amber was often left on her own with no food, but it had remained hidden for six months because the old lady who lived in the flat next door had

My Brother's Secret

been stepping in to help. She'd taken Amber under her wing, looking after her when Petra often disappeared for days on end. It was only when Petra had fallen pregnant again and a midwife had expressed concerns, that she'd finally fallen under Social Service's radar. It had quickly become clear what was going on at home and Amber had been taken into care.

Despite everything that she'd been through in her short life, she was such a sweet girl. It had taken the last few weeks for her to get used to a routine – regular mealtimes, bathtimes and bedtimes. She'd fought against it at first and there had been tantrums, nightmares and lots of wet beds. They were still occurring but less frequently and she was starting to seem more settled.

'It's so lovely to see her with Edie,' I said to Louisa. 'I think being around her is really helping.'

Edie had been the best teacher when it came to showing her how to play. Children who'd experienced neglect like Amber, who, from being babies, hadn't had much stimulation or interaction, weren't able to play creatively. She'd been left in front of the telly for hours on end in a bare, cold flat. When she'd first come to me, I'd shown Amber some toys and she didn't have a clue what to do with them. But she'd watched in fascination as Edie used her imagination to play with dolls, cars or dinosaurs and she'd tried to copy her. It had taken time and perseverance but slowly she was learning how to be a child. Little ones like Amber always made me realise what an important part play has in a child's emotional growth.

'Is Amber going to be with you for long?' asked Louisa.

'I don't know yet,' I shrugged.

Amber's social worker, Harry, had contacted me a few days ago to say that Petra had a sister in the Czech Republic, where she was originally from. She'd told Social Services that she was keen to take Amber and have her go and live with her and her family over there.

They'd just started looking into the possibility. They would have to do all of the usual checks from the UK and link up with the Czech social services, who would go and visit Amber's aunt at home. Amber had never met her aunt, who already had two children of her own.

'It's still being worked out,' I told Louisa. 'But a family member has come forward who might want to take her on.'

'Well, it's lovely to see her and Edie playing so nicely,' she smiled. 'Hopefully she'll be around for a little while yet.'

I stood up from the table and pushed my chair back.

'Right, I'm going to load up the dishwasher,' I said. 'And then I'd better get that cake sorted for the girls.'

I glanced over at Louisa who suddenly looked absolutely exhausted.

'Are you OK, flower?' I asked her. 'You look shattered.'

'Oh yes, I'm fine,' she replied, jumping up. 'I'm just going to nip to the loo.'

She practically ran out of the room and when she came back ten minutes later, she was ashen.

'I'm sorry,' she sighed, 'I think I need to go home. I'm not feeling well at all; I just feel really queasy.'

'Oh, lovey,' I replied. 'Come and sit down and I'll get you a glass of water.'

I led her over to the sofa and she slumped down.

'So when were you going to tell me then?' I asked her, sitting down next to her.

'Tell you what?' she asked innocently.

'That you're pregnant.'

Louisa gave me a weak smile.

'Is it that obvious?' she sighed.

'Well, it is to me,' I said, grinning.

'I was going to tell you but it's still so early,' she told me. 'I'm only a few weeks gone and I feel terrible.'

'Oh, flower, that's wonderful news,' I grinned, giving her a hug. 'I'm so happy for the three of you.'

'Thank you,' she said. 'It's taken a while. We've been trying for months and to be honest, I was starting to worry that it was never going to happen.'

'Edie's going to be thrilled,' I replied.

'I know,' smiled Louisa. 'She's going to be an amazing big sister. I just wish I didn't feel so lousy.'

'It will soon pass,' I reassured her. 'It's a good sign that all those hormones are kicking in.'

I'd suspected for a while that they'd been trying for another baby. I'd noticed a few months ago that Louisa had stopped drinking caffeine and neither she nor Charlie were drinking alcohol. I hadn't said anything as completely understandably, Louisa was quite private about things like that.

'I'm so excited,' I beamed. 'Another little one to love.'

'I know,' she replied. 'I'm worried the flat's too small but we can't afford to move right now.'

'You'll manage' I told her. 'And you've still got all your baby stuff from Edie up in the loft.'

They'd kept Edie's old pram, crib and cot and had been kind enough to lend me a few things over the past few years whenever I'd had a baby to foster.

'That's true,' she nodded.

'Maggie, please will you keep it to yourself for a while,' she added. 'I'm only around seven weeks and I want to wait until we've had our first scan before I tell Edie.'

'Of course,' I said. 'My lips are sealed.'

'I just hope everything's going to be OK,' she added, her brow furrowing with worry.

I could understand her fears. Louisa's first baby – a little boy called Dominic – had died shortly after he was born. At the twenty-week scan, doctors realised he wasn't developing properly in the womb and they were told that he was unlikely to survive to full term. Louisa and Charlie had made the brave decision for her to be induced and Dominic had only lived for five minutes after his birth. It was heart-wrenching seeing how broken they both were for months afterwards. Even though Edie had helped bring the joy back into their lives, I knew Louisa could never relax and enjoy being pregnant until she was holding a healthy baby in her arms.

'It will all be fine,' I told her, patting her hand.

'Let me know if I can look after Edie a little bit more at weekends so you can rest,' I added. 'Amber would definitely be happy to see more of her.'

'Thanks,' she smiled. 'I might take you up on that. I just want to sleep all the time.'

Suddenly the girls came running back into the kitchen demanding cake and sadly we didn't have any more opportunities to chat.

Later that night, after Louisa and Edie had gone, I ran a bath for Amber. My heart felt full of excitement at the thought of my family growing and having another baby to love and treasure.

As I handed Amber a flannel, I wondered to myself if it would be a boy or a girl.

'I love babies,' I said out loud. 'Do you like babies, Amber?'

I said it without thinking and, as soon as the words had left my mouth, I desperately wished I could take them back.

Amber nodded.

'My mummy had a baby in her tummy,' she told me.

Petra's baby, a little boy called Richard, had been born six weeks prematurely after she'd taken heroin throughout her pregnancy. Sadly, I knew the reality of what that looked like from the babies I'd fostered in the past. It was always distressing to see a newborn baby having to go through drug withdrawal in the first few days of their life. I remember going to see one little boy that I was due to foster straight from the hospital. It was horrendous to hear his high-pitched cries and see his tiny, frail legs and arms trembling as his body withdrew from the drug. He'd suffered for months afterwards and had even had seizures which were terrifying to witness.

Richard, who was Amber's half-brother, had spent the past month in hospital being monitored. Harry and I had talked about him with Amber, and tried to explain it to her in an age-appropriate way. It was important for her to see Richard so we'd taken her up to the hospital for a short visit. She'd stared at him shyly in the incubator and stroked his face.

'Where's baby Richard?' Amber asked me now.

'He's in the hospital,' I reminded her. 'Remember we went up to see him? The doctor said he's getting better every day.'

Amber nodded and then carried on splashing about in the bath water.

Thankfully Richard was becoming stronger and the plan was to discharge him soon to another foster carer. Newborn babies tended to find adoptive parents very quickly and easily but with all the paperwork, it could still take a few months. Hopefully Amber would get the chance to see him one last time before he was adopted; it was then up to the adoptive parents whether they chose to stay in touch with her or not.

Sadly, there was no point in Amber having lots of contact sessions with Richard while he was with his foster carers. She would start to build up a bond and a relationship with him and then it would be upsetting for her when he was adopted. There was also the risk his adoptive parents wouldn't want to keep in touch with her.

I could understand it when adoptive families didn't want their child to keep in touch with birth siblings. I'd experienced this a lot especially with the babies and toddlers that I'd fostered. I think as they get older, adoptive parents worry that birth siblings are somehow going to negatively influence their child. They sometimes have a fear that if their child stays in contact with their birth siblings, they'll constantly be reminded of their old life and try to hang on to it, and not fully move on and attach to them. Each case has to be judged independently but generally, I think it's positive for children to maintain that connection to their birth siblings. As they're growing up, it gives them a sense of where they've come from, and helps them to learn about and understand their past and how they came to be in the care system. Some adopters are really keen to keep that contact and I always try to support that if it's in the child's best interests.

Having Amber in Richard's life would be a constant reminder for them of his birth mother and his traumatic start in life. But, particularly as they got older, I felt it was a positive thing for children to have that connection with their biological siblings.

'Is Mummy coming to get me soon?' Amber asked suddenly.

The mention of her baby brother had obviously got her thinking and remembering.

Even though her life with Petra had been chaotic to say the least – she'd often been left home alone in a run-down, cold flat with just biscuits, sweets and crisps to eat – it had still been home to her and 'familiar'.

'Remember Harry told you that Mummy's not able to look after you at the moment,' I told her. 'So you're going to stay here a little while longer with me.'

Social Services had offered Petra the chance to have supervised sessions with Amber but so far, she'd failed to turn up to any of them. Thankfully the contact centre was only a ten-minute drive from my house and Harry had always arranged for Petra to arrive half an hour earlier than us. So he'd always been able to ring me and tell me that she hadn't turned up before I'd set off with Amber. I'd not even told her that we were going to see her mummy as there was nothing worse than having to explain to a child that their birth parent hadn't turned up to see them.

My heart felt heavy with sadness, hearing this little girl asking for her mother and seeing her acceptance as I told her her mother couldn't look after her at the moment.

I read Amber a story – something she'd only recently started to tolerate and sit still for – then tucked her in, as ever hoping for a peaceful night.

As I sat in front of the TV that evening, I smiled to myself as I thought of the new grandchild on the way. Louisa was right – it was going to be a challenge for her and Charlie. They had a small two-bed flat and I knew they'd been saving for a house. Charlie was a mechanic and Louisa was a nanny so they didn't have much spare cash and it was going to take them a while.

I always felt guilty that I couldn't help them out more financially, but fostering is never something that you choose to do for the money. People are often under the misapprehension that foster carers earn hundreds of pounds a week when, in reality, it's much less than the minimum wage and you're on duty 24/7. As a single carer, I just about managed to get by every month but sadly there wasn't much spare to be able to give to Louisa and Charlie. What I could offer was helping out with Edie a bit more so Louisa could rest.

However, worries aside, I couldn't wait for another baby to love and my heart swelled at the thought of my little family growing.

TWO

A Proposition

The following morning, I was still buzzing about Louisa's baby news as I got Amber ready.

I was planning to take her for another session at a local playgroup. She wasn't old enough to go to school yet but I wanted her to spend some time in a childcare setting. It was important for her to get used to being around other children as well as learn how to follow instructions from adults. The previous times we had been there, I'd stayed with her but today I was hoping to leave her for half an hour on her own. Next year, she'd be starting school and it would be a huge shock for her if she hadn't had much chance to mix with her peers.

I was just making breakfast when the phone rang. I thought it might be Amber's social worker Harry ringing with news about her aunt in the Czech Republic.

'Apologies for the early call, Maggie,' said a familiar female voice.

'Oh, hi, Becky,' I said to my supervising social worker. 'How are things with you?'

'Busy but all good,' she told me. 'How's Amber?'

'She's doing really well,' I smiled. 'She's a lot more settled and she's getting on with Edie so that's been nice to see.'

'Aw bless,' she replied. 'I haven't seen Edie for ages – I bet she's looking really grown up now.'

'She is,' I said.

I was so excited about the new baby, it was hard keeping it quiet but I'd promised Louisa that I wouldn't share the news.

'I'm not actually ringing about Amber,' continued Becky, changing the subject. 'I wanted to test the water and see how you'd feel about taking on another placement?'

'Oh,' I replied, surprised.

I put down the toast that I was buttering and sat at the kitchen table so I could concentrate properly.

'You're still on the vacancy list so I thought I'd at least run the idea by you,' she said.

'Absolutely,' I nodded. 'You know I'm always keen to help if I have the room.'

I'd been approved to foster up to three children at a time and I had the space for it. Sometimes, depending on circumstances, or if it was a large sibling group, I was able to get an exemption that meant I could foster more children.

Sadly, local authorities always had more children than there were foster homes available so I'd often have more than one placement with me at a time and I was used to balancing the needs of different children. I imagined it was like being a birth parent: you just got on with it and got used to the juggle. I enjoyed fostering children of different ages at the same time. I liked the variety and if I was ever struggling, I would call on my support system – people like Louisa and my friend Vicky, who was also a single foster carer – to help.

My Brother's Secret

Amber was sleeping in the single bedroom but I also had a large bedroom with bunk beds and a single bed in it, which I used for fostering too.

I felt those first flutters of intrigue that I always did when Becky rang about a new placement.

'So what can you tell me about this little one?' I asked her.

'Actually, there's two of them,' she replied. 'They're brothers and they're not exactly little either.'

She explained that it was two boys – Keegan, eleven, and Cooper, fourteen.

'As you know, older kids are always more difficult to place but I thought I would try you on the off chance as I know you have a soft spot for troubled teenagers.'

'You know me well,' I laughed.

A lot of foster carers wouldn't even consider fostering two older boys but I thrived on older, more problematic, kids. I liked the challenge of trying to work out what their issues were and how I could help them.

She also explained that the boys had a younger brother too – four-year-old Billy.

'Oh, so there's three of them?' I asked, confused.

'No, they've been able to find a foster placement for Billy,' Becky explained. 'But unfortunately that carer didn't want to take on the older boys as well.'

She explained that Social Services realised it was going to be hard to find a carer to take on all three boys, so they'd decided to place Billy and then search for another carer for the older two ones.

If they couldn't find a carer to take them, the only option would be for them to go to a children's home.

'They're keen to avoid that though,' Becky told me. 'Apparently the boys have been through a lot and they'd prefer for them to be placed with a foster carer.'

Children's homes tended to be for kids who struggled in foster care and were too disruptive to live in a home environment.

'Helen, their social worker, is really struggling to place them with any of the carers who work for the local authority,' Becky told me. 'She and I were chatting about the boys and you came to mind straight away.

'Obviously there's no obligation,' she added. 'I completely understand if you decide it's not the right thing for you and I know you've got Amber to think about too. I thought I would try you first just in case you felt like it was something you might consider.'

I knew this wasn't going to be an instant decision.

'I'm not going to say no but I'd like to know a bit more about them first,' I told her. 'As you pointed out, I've got Amber to consider too.'

'Absolutely,' replied Becky.

She paused.

'I'm just about to go to an appointment at a house about ten minutes from you,' she added. 'Why don't I pop round afterwards on my way back to the office? I can say hi to Amber and we can talk it through.'

'That sounds perfect,' I told her. 'I'll make sure the kettle's on.'

As well as finding out more about the two boys, it would be nice to catch up with Becky. I'd been with my fostering agency for years and she'd been my supervising social worker for most of that time. Her role was to be my support and my sounding board. She was the buffer between me and the local

My Brother's Secret

authority, and would check that I was OK. I'd talk to Becky about any issues or problems that I had and she would help me come up with a solution, liaising with social workers or the local authority on my behalf, if needed. We got on well and it was rare for us to get a chance to have a coffee together.

'Becky's coming over later to talk to me,' I told Amber.

She'd met Becky a couple of times over the past few weeks.

'Will she play with me?' asked Amber.

'Not today, flower, because she really needs to talk to me,' I told her. 'But as a special treat, I'll let you pick something to watch on the television.'

'OK,' she grinned.

An hour later, Becky was at the front door.

'Come on in,' I smiled.

'I can't remember the last time I was here,' she said. 'It's been so busy and we seem only to see each other at meetings these days.'

We tended to catch up at the agency or at Social Services.

'Not a lot's changed,' I smiled. 'I still haven't redecorated the kitchen and I always seem to be battling an endless washing and ironing pile.'

'At least it's homely,' she laughed.

'Amber, do you want to watch some cartoons now?' I asked her and she nodded eagerly.

I didn't tend to put the TV on during the day but it would give me and Becky the time to sit and chat without interruption.

Once Amber was settled on the sofa in the front room, I went back into the kitchen and sat down with Becky.

'So,' I smiled, 'what can you tell me about Keegan and Cooper? How have they ended up in the care system?'

'The poor lads have been through a lot,' she sighed.

She explained that their mum, Cheryl, had died of cancer a couple of years ago when the youngest, Billy, was only two.

'Their parents were separated by then but they moved in with their dad, Jason,' she explained. 'Sadly, things slowly deteriorated.'

The boys had come under Social Service's radar when teachers noticed that Keegan and Cooper were coming into school scruffy and unkempt. Their uniform was dirty and smelly and they were hungry and tired.

'It was clear that Jason was struggling to cope but social workers were working with him to try and support him with the boys,' she said.

Becky described how they'd got Billy a nursery place and a social worker was visiting him every few weeks.

'But then a few days ago, Jason just upped and left.'

'What do you mean?' I asked.

Becky explained that he had phoned his social worker and said he was moving to the other side of the country to be with his new girlfriend.

'What about the boys?' I asked.

'Apparently he said his girlfriend already had four kids of her own and there wasn't room for the boys at her house.'

I was flabbergasted.

'So he just left his three sons?'

'Yep,' nodded Becky. 'The social worker went round and tried to talk it through with him but he just got up and walked out.'

She described how he'd already cleared the flat and packed all the boys' belongings in bin bags. Social Services hadn't been able to get hold of him since.

My Brother's Secret

Becky said the boys hadn't even been aware that he was going.

The image of three boys standing there with all their worldly belongings in bin bags, watching their father walk out on them was heartbreaking.

'I suppose the only saving grace is that at least he told Social Services he was going,' I shrugged.

Some parents just disappeared, leaving their children on their own to fend for themselves.

'So where are the boys now?' I asked.

'There wasn't any family around who was willing to take them so we've managed to place them both with an emergency foster carer for now.'

Some foster carers only did emergency work. If social workers needed to remove children suddenly or in the middle of the night, or if police were interviewing a child, that's when emergency carers came in. They were always on call and tended to work two weeks on and two weeks off. They'd take children without any notice, sometimes for just a few hours or at the most, a few days. That gave social workers a bit of breathing space while they found the right placement for them. It wasn't for me but some carers I knew enjoyed it because it meant they didn't become emotionally attached to a child. You were just there to give them a safe but temporary place to stay.

'The emergency carer can only take them for a couple of days,' added Becky. 'So Social Services are keen to place them.'

'Those poor boys,' I sighed.

It never failed to amaze me how some parents just abandoned their children. These three boys would still be grieving for their mother and must be feeling so rejected and alone.

'Do you know what they're like?' I asked Becky.

'I haven't met them but I've spoken to their social worker Helen and she sent me their case notes. She described Keegan as a quiet, well-behaved boy who was doing well at school Cooper sounds like the exact opposite,' she sighed. 'Very disruptive in class, cheeky, gets into fights. He's clearly a child who likes to push back against boundaries and authority.'

I nodded.

'I think they're keen to try and keep them together in the hope that some of Keegan's calmness will rub off on Cooper and his behaviour will start to settle.'

'They've been through a lot; it's not surprising there are a few issues,' I said.

'I'm not going to sugar-coat it,' said Becky. 'If you decide to take them on, it's going to be challenging, particularly with Cooper.'

She paused.

'And it's whether you feel you can cope with that and Amber too. So I completely understand if you decide it's not for you.'

I didn't know what to think. These boys had been through a lot and I could understand why Cooper was pushing buttons and showing some challenging behaviour. But could I deal with that on top of Amber's needs too? But there was also the chance that things would work out with her aunt and she could be off to live in the Czech Republic in a few weeks.

'Can I sleep on it and get back to you in the morning?' I asked.

'Of course,' Becky nodded. 'I know it's a big decision.'

Becky and I chatted for a while longer before she had to get back to the office.

'I promise, I'll ring you first thing,' I assured her. 'I know Social Services need to find a solution.'

For the rest of the day, I was engrossed in my thoughts, weighing everything up in my mind.

I took Amber to the playgroup and to my surprise, she was happy for me to leave her.

I only had half an hour so I decided to sit in my car and give my friend Vicky a call. She was my sounding board and my shoulder to cry on, as I was hers. I trusted her opinion as she'd been a foster carer for over twenty years, like me.

'What is it, Maggie?' she asked when I rang. 'You sound hassled.'

'I'm fine,' I replied. 'I've just got a bit of a dilemma.'

I told her about Cooper and Keegan.

'What are your worries?' she asked. 'Do you think you'd struggle to cope with balancing the needs of a four-year-old and two older children?'

'I've fostered little ones and teens in the past and actually I think it can work quite well,' I told her.

Younger children often helped to soften teens and they would end up playing with them. Plus little ones went to bed early, leaving time for me to spend with older children.

'I think you've answered your own question,' Vicky told me and in my heart I knew what I wanted to do.

When we got home from the playgroup, I called Becky.

'I thought you were going to call me tomorrow?' she replied.

'There's no need – I've already made up my mind,' I said firmly. 'I'm going to say yes. I'd like to foster Keegan and Cooper.'

THREE

New Arrivals

Now I'd made a decision, everything suddenly started moving very quickly.

'I'll call their social worker Helen and she'll be in touch,' Becky told me. 'She might even want to bring them round this evening.'

'Tonight?' I asked. 'I understand if there's no other option but please could I have this evening to get their bedrooms ready and sort everything out?'

'I'll do my best,' replied Becky.

Thankfully she messaged me back to say Helen was happy to bring them round first thing the following morning.

A lot of the time, children did arrive with only a few hours' notice. However, I knew these boys were safe with another carer and it was good to buy myself a little bit more time so I felt I was properly prepared.

I tackled the bedroom first and gave it a quick hoover and dust. There was already clean bedding on the beds but I changed the duvet covers to blue stripey ones as I worried the purple ones I currently had on might be a bit too girly for them.

Amber looked on curiously.

'We've got two big boys coming to stay with us,' I told her. 'Their names are Keegan and Cooper.'

'Will they sleep in my room?' she asked.

'No, flower, they're going to sleep in here,' I told her. 'That's why I'm getting everything nice and tidy for them.'

'Are they coming now?' she asked.

'No, not until the morning,' I replied.

In typical four-year-old fashion, she just nodded and seemed to accept it instantly, without question.

Once I was happy the bedroom was sorted, I got all of the basics out of my cupboard. I'd bulk-buy things when they were on offer so I had a constant supply of toothbrushes, towels, flannels and other toiletries all ready and waiting for when I needed them.

I wasn't sure how much stuff Keegan and Cooper were going to have with them but I knew I could dig out some emergency pyjamas and clothes if needed until I could take them to the shops.

For the rest of the day, I was filled with a feeling of anticipation. I always had a few nerves the day before a new placement arrived. I couldn't help but wonder if it was going to work out and if these boys were going to be happy with me.

I also wanted to sort out some jobs that I'd planned to tackle in the next few days but I wouldn't have time for now as I would need to focus on Keegan and Cooper. I quickly wrapped a birthday present I'd bought for Charlie, sent my good friend Graham an email as he'd been staying with his sister in Australia for the past few months, and did some paperwork from my agency that I needed to clear.

I also gave Vicky a quick call.

'Thanks for your advice,' I told her. 'I decided to bite the bullet and go for it.'

'That's great news,' she replied. 'When do they arrive?'

'Tomorrow,' I said. 'I'm running round like mad trying to get everything sorted.'

'I know what that's like,' she laughed. 'Good luck, it'll be fine.'

'I hope so,' I shrugged.

That night, I started to get Amber ready for bed much earlier than usual. I hoped it wasn't going to be one of those long nights where she was up and down and tricky to settle, as I wanted to try and get a good night's sleep ahead of the following day.

Thankfully, it was if she'd read my mind and she was the calmest she'd ever been. She splashed around happily in the bath and let me help her get into her pyjamas. She was getting used to having a bedtime routine and seemed to be enjoying it. Children liked predictability; it helped to make them feel safe. It had taken a few weeks, but Amber had now learnt that after tea and clearing up, it was bath, teeth brushing, then story time and bed.

As I read her a story on the chair in her room, I felt Amber lean back against me, the weight of her little body squishing into mine. I could feel her breathing deeply as I turned the pages of the book. She wasn't wriggling around to get off my lap or trying to rip the pages like she'd done when she'd arrived a couple of months ago. I realised it was the first time I'd seen her truly relax since she'd come to my house. When children have suffered neglect, they're often on hyperalert. They're constantly fidgety and distracted and find it difficult to concentrate on one thing and be still.

I thought about all the times Amber must have been left home alone before her elderly neighbour had taken her in. I couldn't imagine the fear she must have felt on those nights in a cold, dark flat; hungry, tired and waiting for her mummy to come home. I was so proud of how far she'd come.

I closed the book.

'Did you like *The Gruffalo*?' I asked her, stroking her long brown hair.

Amber had told me she'd never had stories read to her before, so I was starting with all of the picture book favourites I'd read to other foster children over the years.

She nodded, her eyes already heavy with sleep.

I felt a pang in my stomach as I wondered what our evenings would look like when Keegan and Cooper arrived the following day. I hoped I'd still be able to devote enough time to Amber as she was really relishing it now she'd got used to things a bit more. I still hadn't heard back from her social worker Harry with any news about her aunt. I reminded myself to chase that up over the next few days.

Thanks to Amber, I got the early night that I'd wanted. As I climbed into bed, I suddenly felt exhausted but I just lay there in the darkness, unable to sleep. My mind was churning with a mixture of feelings, worrying whether I'd done the right thing by taking these boys on but, at the same time, looking forward to the challenge.

★

My Brother's Secret

I managed to get a few hours' sleep and the following morning I was up bright and early. I didn't know what time the boys were arriving but I wanted to be dressed and ready because I knew from past experience that social workers had a habit of arriving first thing.

My instincts proved right. Just after nine, there was a loud knock at the front door.

'Is it them?' Amber asked, wide-eyed, and I nodded.

She scurried after me as I went to let them in.

I opened it to find a woman with long dark hair who looked to be in her forties, wearing a floral dress and a cardigan and holding up her Social Services lanyard.

'Hi, Maggie,' she smiled. 'I'm Helen from Social Services. And this is Keegan and Cooper.'

Standing next to her, clutching a bin bag each, were two boys. I could tell who was who straight away. They had the same short brown hair, shaved round the sides, and identical clear blue eyes but there was a big difference in their builds. Cooper was tall and stocky whereas Keegan was slight and several inches shorter. They were both wearing grubby grey tracksuit bottoms and faded grey sweatshirts.

'Hi, boys,' I said. 'Come on in.'

Keegan gave me a weak smile of acknowledgement but Cooper didn't say a word and stared straight at me with a bored look on his face.

'Come in,' I told them, ushering them into the hallway.

Amber came up shyly behind me and grabbed my hand.

'Amber, this is Keegan and Cooper,' I told her. 'They've come to stay with us for a while.'

'I'm four,' she told them. 'Do you want to play with my toys?'

They both looked very awkward and didn't know what to say to her in return.

'Why don't you all come through to the kitchen and I can get you a drink,' I suggested. 'Have you had any breakfast, boys?'

They shook their heads.

'Well, I'm sure I can rustle something up,' I replied.

'Maggie, I'm so sorry but I'm afraid I've got to rush back to the office,' Helen told me apologetically. 'But I'm sure Keegan and Cooper will be able to answer any questions that you might have.'

I was surprised that Helen was leaving so soon, particularly as she was a social worker whom I hadn't dealt with before. I thought she would have at least stayed for a cup of tea to make sure the boys were OK and settled.

'Oh, before I forget, I just need to get your signature on a couple of forms,' she said, quickly whipping them out of her bag and shoving them into my hand.

They were delegated responsibility forms that meant I had permission to seek medical care for the boys or take them to the optician or dentist. It was one of the first bits of paperwork you had to sign at the beginning of any placement.

Helen handed me a pen and I leant on the table in the hallway and quickly scribbled my signature. Then she whipped it away and put it in her bag. She was halfway down the front path when she suddenly stopped and turned around.

'Oh, before I forget, I've emailed you the details of their school,' she called. 'I'd really like them to go in tomorrow as they haven't been for the past few days and I think it would be good for them to have some normality and routine.'

'OK,' I nodded.

A few seconds later, Helen got into her car and drove off. The boys were still standing awkwardly in the hallway with Amber staring them up and down.

'Let's all go through to the kitchen,' I said.

I could see they didn't know what to do with themselves.

'Why don't you put your stuff down,' I told them, 'and come and sit at the table.'

They put their bin bags on the floor and wandered over.

'How about I do you both a bacon sandwich?' I asked. 'Do you fancy that?'

'That'd be good,' replied Keegan and Cooper shrugged.

'Amber, do you want to come and help me?' I asked her, keen to stop her staring at the boys.

I distracted her by giving her some plastic bowls and beakers to put away in the cupboard while I put some bacon under the grill and poured out some glasses of orange juice.

Keegan looked around nervously while Cooper lay with his head on the table.

'Are you tired, Cooper?' I asked him.

'Yeah, that woman made us get up so f***ing early this morning,' he sighed.

'We've got a little one in the house, so can we cut out the swearing please?' I told him.

'I'll say what I want,' he scoffed.

'Well, it's something I'm going to pick you up on every time,' I replied. 'So you're going to get fed up of me moaning about it.'

I glanced over at Amber but she was still engrossed in her task so I was pretty sure that she hadn't heard him.

I put the bacon sandwiches down and both boys tucked in hungrily. Amber and I had already had breakfast so I sat on the floor with her and did a jigsaw as I didn't want the boys to feel like they were under a microscope.

'Why don't you get your stuff and I'll show you where you're sleeping?' I said when they'd finished.

'You've got bunk beds in your room,' Amber told them proudly.

They grabbed their bin bags and I led them up the stairs, Amber scampering after them eagerly.

I wanted to try and keep her occupied while I showed the boys their bedroom. Because she'd enjoyed her bedtime story so much the previous night, I'd filled up the little bookcase in her room with more picture books.

'Why don't you pick a story for me to read to you tonight while I go and show Keegan and Cooper their room?' I asked her.

'OK,' nodded Amber. 'I might pick *Stick Man* this time.'

'Good choice,' I smiled.

Both boys were still very quiet as we walked down the landing towards their bedroom.

'You two must be used to four-year-olds as Helen was telling me you've got a little brother,' I said. 'Billy, isn't it?'

'No, he ain't with us no more,' snapped Cooper.

'Another lady took him,' Keegan added.

'Has Helen talked to you about seeing him?' I asked them. 'She could arrange what we call a contact session with Billy where you all meet up and spend some time together.'

Cooper shook his head.

'She didn't mention nothing like that,' he said.

'When I speak to Helen later, I'll ask her if we can have the number of Billy's foster carer and maybe we could organise a phone call with him?'

'Whatever,' shrugged Cooper.

I pushed open their bedroom door.

'This is where you'll be sleeping,' I told them.

They looked around.

'As you can see, there are bunk beds but if one of you doesn't want to be in those, there's a single bed too,' I told them. 'So I'll let you decide between you where you want to sleep.'

Neither of them said anything. They looked so lost and shell-shocked, my heart went out to them.

'How about I help you unpack?' I said cheerily.

Keegan picked up his bin bag and tipped it all out onto the floor.

There wasn't much and what was in there was crumpled, creased and stained. There were just a few tatty-looking T-shirts, ripped tracksuit bottoms and faded jeans.

Cooper threw down his bin bag and flopped on the bed.

As I glanced at Keegan's stuff, I couldn't see anything that looked like a school uniform.

'Have you got your uniform for school?' I asked them both.

'What, you're really gonna make us go to school?' sighed Cooper.

'Here's mine,' said Keegan, picking up creased trousers and a grubby-looking white shirt out of the pile on the floor.

'Cooper, what about yours?' I asked, turning to him.

'Dunno,' he sighed. 'It might be in there.'

He gestured to the bin bag he hadn't unpacked yet. I guessed they didn't have any other shoes besides the worn trainers they'd turned up in either.

'What about school bags?' I asked. 'Have you got pencil cases and pens and things?'

They both looked at me blankly.

'I just borrow that stuff from my mates,' said Cooper.

'That's nice of your friends but it's always good to have your own things,' I told him.

I couldn't knowingly send them both off to secondary school without everything they needed.

'It looks like we're going to need a quick shopping trip, boys,' I told them.

I put the rest of their clothes into the washing machine then I bundled them and Amber into the car and we headed to the local retail park where I went into M&S and picked up two plain white shirts and two pairs of black trousers for each of them.

'Do you wear blazers or jumpers at your school?' I asked them.

I knew I'd probably have to buy those the following day from either the school or a special uniform shop.

'Jumpers,' replied Keegan. 'But you don't need to buy them – the teacher just gives us one from lost property.'

'I ain't wearing no sh*t smelly jumpers,' scoffed Cooper.

'Cooper, remember I said I'm not going to tolerate that kind of language,' I told him and he rolled his eyes.

I quickly changed the subject and explained that I'd need to go up to their school tomorrow and give them my contact information.

'I can get you some jumpers then,' I told them.

I also got them to choose some boxer shorts and socks, and a plain black rucksack each and some smart black school shoes. Then we went to a stationery shop and got pens, pencils and rulers.

'You should both be all sorted now,' I smiled.

My Brother's Secret

It was a big outlay for me and I knew that tomorrow I needed to email their social worker Helen and explain that I'd had to kit them out with everything for school. As part of the weekly allowance I got for each placement, a small part of it was intended for clothing. However, this was meant to replace the odd item and didn't account for kitting a child out from scratch. Lots of carers ended up out of pocket when they had to clothe children who arrived with hardly anything and, the truth was, I couldn't afford it.

When we got back, I made us all some lunch then the boys went up to their bedroom. I wanted to leave them on their own for a bit to settle in.

I played with Amber and did some tidying up. I made an early dinner as I knew the boys would be tired and overwhelmed after today. As we all sat round the table, both Keegan and Cooper were very quiet as they shovelled spaghetti bolognese into their mouths.

'Has that woman said anything about Dad yet?' asked Cooper.

'Do you mean Helen, your social worker?' I asked and he nodded.

'I'm not sure to be honest, flower,' I told him. 'Helen and I didn't really have time to chat today but I'm hoping to catch up with her tomorrow.'

I hadn't heard anything else from her for the entire day. I would have expected at least a quick call to see how everything was going and check on how the boys were.

'I'm sure Helen's been trying to get hold of your dad to let him know where you are,' I said.

'He's at his girlfriend's,' said Keegan.

'Have you met his girlfriend?' I asked them.

'Yeah, but she didn't like us,' muttered Cooper. 'She's got her own kids so she said she ain't going to take on any more.'

'Dad just went anyway,' said Keegan.

'That must be really tough,' I soothed.

Neither of them said a word, they just carried on eating.

They both suddenly looked so young and scared and my heart broke for them and how rejected they must be feeling.

FOUR

Pushing the Boundaries

That evening I could tell the boys were still tired from their early start. While I put Amber to bed, they went back to their bedroom. I was fine with that as I wanted their room to feel like their safe space and somewhere they could retreat to.

I gave Amber a bath and once she'd got into her pyjamas, it was story time. She was a lot more fidgety tonight and kept interrupting me by asking questions.

'When will Keeper and Coogan go to bed?' she asked and I couldn't help but laugh.

'I think you mean Keegan and Cooper,' I smiled. 'They're big boys so they'll be going to bed a bit later than you.'

'I'll be fast asleep by then,' she nodded.

'I hope so,' I told her.

Every day I was seeing more of what a sweet little girl she was and she melted my heart.

Once Amber was finally settled, I went to check on the boys. I gently knocked on the door before I opened it. They were both lying on their beds – Keegan on the single bed and Cooper on the top bunk.

'How are you doing?' I asked them both.

Cooper shut his eyes and ignored me and Keegan shrugged.

'I bet you're shattered,' I said. 'Why don't you both have a shower and it will save time in the morning? Afterwards you can come downstairs for a hot drink and a biscuit if you want, before bed.'

Cooper refused to move but I took Keegan to the bathroom and showed him how the shower worked and where the clean towels were.

'Help yourself to whatever toiletries you need,' I told him.

Neither of them came downstairs but just after nine-thirty, I popped my head back around their door. They were both still curled up on their beds and looked exhausted.

'It's bedtime now, boys,' I said. 'I hope you both sleep OK. Shout if you need anything.'

By 10.30 p.m., the whole house was silent so I decided to head to bed myself. It had been a busy day and I was pleased the boys seemed to have settled OK and everything was calm.

I'd set my alarm for 6 a.m. as I wanted to make sure that I was up before the boys and Amber so I could get everything ready before I dropped them at school. It was at least a half an hour drive from my house. Amber woke up half an hour later and at seven I went to wake Keegan and Cooper.

'Boys come on,' I told them. 'It's time to get up. You need to get ready for school.'

Keegan sat up and started to get out of bed.

'Good lad,' I told him. 'Come on, Cooper, otherwise you're going to be late.'

'I don't care,' he snapped. 'Go away. I ain't f***ing going.'

My Brother's Secret

I chose to ignore him as I didn't want to get into a stand-off when he was still half asleep.

'As soon as you're both up and dressed, come down and I'll get you some breakfast,' I said.

As I went downstairs, I was filled with dread at the thought of Cooper refusing to go to school. I could have responded to him there and then and tried to persuade him but sometimes by walking away, it can give children the opportunity to pause and change their thought process. Also, I didn't want to start an argument in his bedroom. I wanted that to be his private space and somewhere he felt safe and secure.

I told myself if he didn't come down, I would cross that bridge when I came to it.

I'd fostered children who were school refusers before and it was always very difficult as you couldn't physically make them go. All you could do was talk to them and try to find out why they didn't want to go and if there was a problem, and work with their social worker to see if we could resolve it. For many neglected children, school was a refuge and somewhere they wanted to be. It was their routine and their safety net from the chaos and instability of their home lives.

'Don't get ahead of yourself, Maggie,' I told myself.

There was nothing to suggest Cooper was a school refuser and Helen hadn't mentioned it. Sometimes kids, especially teenagers, didn't like being woken up in the mornings and we weren't all chirpy first thing.

Fifteen minutes later, Keegan came down in his new white shirt and black trousers.

'You look really smart,' I told him. 'Help yourself to some breakfast and then I'll drive you to school.'

He nodded.

'Cooper's just coming,' he said.

I tried not to show it but I was hugely relieved to hear this.

Ten minutes later, Cooper finally appeared dressed in his school uniform. He threw his rucksack on the floor and sighed as he sat down at the table.

Both boys shovelled down big bowls of cereal in silence, watched intently by Amber.

She'd brought a doll down from her bedroom and had put it on the table next to her.

'Oh no, my dolly's shoe's come off,' she cried.

She turned to Cooper.

'Can you put it back on for me?' she asked him.

I thought he was going to tell her to get lost but he nodded.

'OK,' he said and he patiently put it back on while Amber looked on adoringly.

I glanced at the clock.

'Right then, boys, we'd better go,' I said.

Everyone was quiet in the car and I was busy concentrating on the roads as I hadn't been to this area before.

We were twenty minutes in, when Cooper suddenly leant forwards.

'Can you stop?' he asked abruptly. 'I wanna get out and walk.'

'Are you sure?' I asked him. 'We're still at least five minutes away from the school.'

'Yep, I ain't being seen dead being dropped off by you,' he sighed.

Luckily I had a thick skin when it came to teenagers! I pulled over and he got out, slamming the car door behind

My Brother's Secret

him. As I watched him walk off, I wasn't particularly worried. I was going into school anyway so I knew they'd be able to tell me if he hadn't turned up for registration.

'Keegan, do you want me to drop you a bit closer?' I asked him.

'Yeah,' he nodded. 'That'd be good.'

Keegan was much quieter and meeker compared to Cooper and his bolshy attitude.

The school car park was for staff and teachers and there was a barrier across it so I pulled into a side street.

'Is this OK for you, lovey?' I asked him.

'Yep,' he nodded.

He got out and started walking away.

'Have a good day,' I called. 'I'll come and pick you both up later.'

'Thanks,' he said, turning round. 'I'll tell Cooper.'

I'd made sure they both had my number and address written in their planners before they'd left that morning.

Amber was still sitting patiently in the back.

'I've just got to go into the school office,' I told her. 'And then I promise we'll go to a Stay and Play afterwards, OK?'

She nodded.

Amber and I walked into the school grounds and we were buzzed into the building. I went to the front desk and explained who I was.

'I wanted to give you my name and details as the contact for Keegan and Cooper,' I told the woman on reception.

'Oh yes, the social worker rang us the other day and told us they'd gone into care,' she told me. 'So sad,' she added.

'It is,' I nodded.

She handed me a form to fill in.

'You're a brave woman taking on Cooper,' she told me. 'He's trouble, that one.'

'He's been fine so far,' I told her, trying to avoid getting into a conversation about it.

'Just you wait,' she shrugged. 'So different from his brother. We never hear a peep from him.'

It was irritating but I didn't want to start openly discussing Cooper's behaviour in the school reception for anyone to hear.

'Can we go to the Stay and Play now?' asked Amber as she skipped along next to me as we left the school.

'Course we can, lovey,' I smiled. 'You've been really patient.'

The Stay and Play was in a church hall and it was one that I'd taken Amber to every week since she'd been with me. She was familiar with the space and some of the other children and she'd really grown in confidence. As soon as we walked in, she rushed over to the sand and water table.

I was just about to make myself a cup of tea when my phone rang.

It was Becky.

I glanced over at Amber who seemed happy, so I sat on a plastic chair and answered it.

'I was just ringing to check how things went yesterday,' she asked.

I talked her through what we'd done.

'I had to take the boys shopping as they didn't have anything they needed for school,' I told her. 'Then the rest of the afternoon was really quiet.'

'And how was Cooper?' she asked.

'We had a bit of swearing, which I pulled him up on, and lots of attitude but nothing major,' I replied. 'But you know as well as I do that often it takes a few weeks or even months before their true behaviour comes out.'

There hadn't been any of the disruptive behaviour from Cooper that Becky had warned me about but I knew this was what was known as the honeymoon period. When children first arrived at a new carer's, you never had a true picture of who they really were. It tended to come out later when the kids felt safe.

'I keep thinking about all they've been through and my heart aches for them,' I said.

'They did ask about their dad and if anyone had heard from him,' I added. 'I didn't know what to say.'

'You need to talk to Helen about that,' replied Becky.

'I wish I could,' I told her.

I explained that I hadn't heard a thing from Helen since she'd dropped them off the previous morning.

'That is strange,' said Becky. 'I would've thought she'd have been in touch by now.'

I told her that the boys had been asking about their little brother Billy and I'd mentioned the possibility of seeing him or at least having a phone call with him.

'That seems fair enough,' replied Becky. "I'm sure Social Services can arrange that.'

She promised to chase Helen up and get her to ring me with an update.

'And how's Amber been with them?' she asked.

'She's been fine,' I told her. 'She's obsessed with both of them and doesn't leave their side. It's quite sweet really.'

After I'd put the phone down to Becky, I felt a lot better. It made such a difference being able to talk things through with someone.

I enjoyed a moment of peace with a cup of tea and a Hobnob while Amber played.

After an hour of running round the church hall, I could see Amber was getting tired.

'Let's head home for some lunch now,' I told her.

On the way back, we popped into the supermarket to get some sausages so I could do bangers and mash for tea.

As I walked in the front door, my mobile started ringing in my bag. I quickly fished it out.

'Maggie, it's Helen,' said a voice. 'I'm so sorry I haven't been in touch – it's been crazy here. How are the boys?'

I gave her a quick rundown.

'Cooper's been a bit tricky but nothing I haven't been able to manage,' I told her. 'We've had some bad language.'

'Oh, I can imagine,' she sighed. 'I had it all in the car yesterday.'

I also mentioned their little brother Billy.

'Is there any possibility you could ask the foster carer who's got Billy whether we can have their phone number so the boys can ring him?'

'I can see,' she said. 'Although they're probably not going to get much out of a four-year-old.'

'At least it's a start, until we can organise contact,' I said.

I appreciated the boys had just arrived so it could be a week or so until contact could be arranged with Billy. It wasn't the same priority as it was with children seeing birth parents.

'Have you heard anything from their dad?' I asked her.

'No, nothing,' replied Helen. 'We keep calling his mobile but he hasn't got back to us. We want to let him know how the boys are and where they are in case he decides he wants to see them.'

I couldn't understand how you could live your life with your children for so long and then one day just get up and walk out on them, and not want any contact with them or to know if they were OK. It could have been guilt but who knew what was going on in Jason's mind?

Helen explained that her manager was talking to the police about Jason to see if they were intending to charge him with child abandonment.

'Is it abandonment if he told you he was leaving?' I asked.

'I don't honestly know,' sighed Helen. 'It's a bit of a grey area.'

She explained that if he eventually signed on for benefits then he would pop back up on the system and they would be able to contact him.

After lunch, as Amber was tired, I let her watch a little bit of TV while I did some tidying. I went into the boys' room. It smelt a bit stuffy so I drew the curtains and opened the top window. I picked their pyjamas up off the floor and made their beds for them.

The afternoon sped by and it was soon time to drive over and pick up them up from school. As I drove past the main entrance, I could see pupils streaming out of the front gates.

I pulled into the same side street where I'd parked that morning and I could see Keegan was already waiting. My heart sank when there was no sign of Cooper.

'Hi, lovey,' I said. 'Where's your brother.'

'He said he ain't coming and he'll get back later.'

'Did he say where he was going?' I asked him.

'Dunno,' shrugged Keegan.

I tried not to worry at this stage. He'd have to get a couple of buses but I hoped Cooper would work out the route back to my house. I knew he had my address and phone number if he got stuck, and the boys already had a bus pass each.

As soon as we got back, Keegan went up to his bedroom. I played with Amber for a while and encouraged her to do some drawing with me, one of the things she'd never done before because of her mum's chaotic lifestyle. Ahead of school, I was trying to improve her dexterity and fine motor skills and get her used to holding a crayon or a pen in her hand.

By five thirty, there was still no sign of Cooper so I messaged Helen.

Cooper hasn't come back from school yet. I'm going to give it until 7 and then I'll ring my agency.

I knew that because of his age, my agency would probably want me to give it until at least 8 p.m. before I phoned the police.

All I could do was carry on as normal so I started peeling potatoes for the mash for dinner.

By half past six, the sausages were cooked, the mash was steaming and the beans were bubbling away on the hob.

'Dinnertime,' I called to Amber and Keegan.

We couldn't wait around all night and were going to have to eat without him.

When we'd finished dinner and there was still no sign of Cooper, I started preparing myself for a long night.

'Where's Cooper?' Amber asked anxiously as I got her out of the bath that night.

My Brother's Secret

'Oh, he'll be back soon,' I told her. 'He's seeing a friend.'

I'd just put her to bed and was walking down the stairs, when there was a loud knock at the front door.

I opened it to find Cooper standing there.

'Alright,' he said, sauntering into the hallway.

Keen not to disturb Amber, we walked through to the kitchen.

'Where have you been?' I asked him. 'It's after seven.'

'Out and about,' he shrugged.

'Cooper, I need you to come back after school; otherwise you need to tell me if you've got other plans,' I told him firmly. 'I didn't know where you were or who you were with.'

'So?' he sighed.

'At the end of the day I'm your foster carer and it's my responsibility to make sure you're OK. If I don't know where you are, then I don't know that you're safe and OK.'

'I'm f***ing fourteen,' he hissed.

'I know how old you are,' I replied. 'I still need to know where you are and what you're doing and ideally you'll be back for dinner at six.'

'B***h,' he muttered under his breath before turning and storming out.

I heard him running up the stairs followed by the thud of his bedroom door slamming.

I padded upstairs and checked that Amber hadn't been disturbed by the commotion. As I peeped around her door, I could see that thankfully she was fast asleep.

I went back downstairs and made a cup of tea. I wasn't going to go and try to talk to Cooper. Often children are disruptive because they want you to react and they feed off that. So if I'd said to Cooper, 'Don't speak to me like that,' he would have probably come back at me and it would have developed into a full-blown row. But because I didn't react to him, he couldn't argue with me and it instantly diffused the situation.

Even though I didn't want a row, I wasn't going to back down. It was important to set boundaries right from the start in any placement. Cooper had come into my house and although he might not like it, this was how I expected our evenings to pan out. I was happy for him to do things after school sometimes and there was some flexibility there, just as long as I knew where he was.

I liked to try and make sure we ate together as much as possible, even if it wasn't every single night. I knew that children, teenagers included, thrived on routine and continuity. Consistency created stability and Cooper and Keegan very much needed that in their lives right now.

Later on, Keegan came down.

'Can I get a drink?' he asked.

'Course you can,' I told him. 'Do you think your brother wants one too or something to eat?'

'No, he's sulking,' he told me.

'When you go up, let him know there's a drink down here if he wants one or some dinner,' I replied.

But he didn't come down. I knocked on their door before I went to bed. Cooper was lying on his side facing the wall and didn't turn round.

'Night night, boys, sleep well. See you in the morning,' I told them.

He didn't say a word or even acknowledge me.

It was late and I wanted a peaceful night. Perhaps Cooper had needed to vent his frustrations and get it out of his system?

At the end of the day, it was the boys' first time back at school after their dad had walked out on them. At the heart of all this, there was a boy who was probably missing his dad and hopefully, as time passed, things would start to settle down.

FIVE

Reconnecting

By the next morning, I was pleased to see that Cooper seemed a lot calmer. I wasn't going to back down though, so on the way out of the door to school, I reminded him of the rules.

'Cooper, if you want to do something after school then remember, please let me know as I need to know where you are,' I told him.

'The same goes for you too, Keegan,' I added. 'If you want to go to a friend's house or something then just tell me.'

Cooper burst out laughing.

'What, this loser?' he scoffed. 'He's a weirdo and he ain't got no friends. He just stays in his room doing his homework.'

'Shut up,' snapped Keegan but Cooper laughed.

'Hey, that's enough, boys,' I told them.

It was the first time that I'd seen bad feeling between the brothers.

Amber looked bemused by the whole thing.

Thankfully everyone was quiet on the drive to school and it was a relief when the boys got out of the car.

'Can we go to Stay and Play again?' asked Amber from the back seat.

'Not today I'm afraid, sweetie,' I told her. 'Harry's coming round to see you.'

Harry had been the social worker for a couple of children that I'd fostered in the past and I liked him. He was very easy-going and he always respected my opinion. He was a calm, gentle man in his thirties who wore cords and lumberjack shirts and had horn-rimmed glasses that kept slipping down his nose.

Amber didn't look too enthralled by the idea.

'Me want Stay and Play,' she sighed.

'I promise I'll take you another day,' I told her.

Harry had messaged that morning to say he wanted to pop round and talk to me. When a social worker took the time out of their hectic schedule to come round and see you, it normally meant they had something significant they wanted to discuss. I knew it must be about Amber's aunt.

In my experience, ordinarily you could never rely on social workers to turn up when they said they were going to but Harry was there at 10 a.m. on the dot.

'Come on in,' I told him. 'I've just put the kettle on.'

'I'm not going to say no to a cup of tea,' he smiled.

Amber was playing in the garden so Harry wandered out to say hello to her.

'How's the new placement going?' he asked, coming back in.

Before they offered me the placement, my agency would have checked with Harry that he was OK with me taking on the boys while Amber was in my care.

'OK,' I said, as I filled up two mugs from the teapot. 'It's only been a few days so we're all still finding our feet.'

'And how's Amber been with the older boys?'

'She's fascinated by them,' I said. 'She practically follows them around.'

'That's sweet,' smiled Harry.

We sat down at the kitchen table to have our tea.

'So what did you want to talk to me about?' I asked him.

Harry glanced outside at Amber. The patio doors were open but I could see she was engrossed in moving around some stones that we'd painted and put outside.

'It's OK, she can't hear us from out there,' I told him.

Harry explained they'd been in touch with Social Services in the Czech Republic and they'd been to see Petra's sister, Martina.

'They've done a couple of home visits and the usual checks and so far, everything looks good,' he said.

He explained that both Martina and her husband worked, their children seemed happy and they had a spare room that Amber could have.

'By all accounts, they're a nice, stable family.'

'It sounds ideal,' I nodded. 'So what happens now?'

Harry said the next step was for Martina to come over to the UK for at least a week to get to know Amber.

'Then if everything goes to plan, at the end of that she will go back to the Czech Republic with her,' he added.

'I assume that's going to take a while to organise?' I asked.

'We're actually looking at doing it in the next few weeks,' he said. 'Martina and her husband seem very committed. She's asked to take some unpaid leave from her job and she's keen to come over and meet Amber as soon as possible.'

'Oh wow,' I sighed. 'That seems so quick.'

'Obviously we need to do a bit of work with Amber first and tell her what's going to happen so she can get used to the idea.'

Harry explained that they'd organise a hotel for Martina and the idea was that by the end of the week, hopefully Amber would feel comfortable enough to stay overnight with her.

I was happy that Amber had this opportunity but I was apprehensive too. It was a lot of change going to live in a different country with a relative that she didn't know. I could see how much she'd settled and progressed in the few short months that she'd been with me and I hoped that would continue.

'I really hope she's going to be OK with it all,' I sighed.

'You've really grown fond of her, haven't you?' asked Harry and I nodded.

'Shall I call her in and you can have a chat to her now?' I asked him.

'I don't see why not,' he said.

I went outside to find Amber digging in the soil where she'd found a worm.

'Why don't you come on in and we'll get those hands of yours washed?' I said. 'Then I'll get you some juice and a biscuit and you can have a chat to Harry.'

I finally got her sat down at the table. While she chomped on her biscuit, Harry started to talk.

'Amber, you know how your mummy can't look after you at the moment?'

She nodded.

'Well, we've been taking to Mummy's sister, Martina, about what's been happening.'

My Brother's Secret

Her face flickered with recognition.

'Aunty Tina?' she asked.

'Oh, do you know your aunty?' I questioned.

'I've seen her on a picture Mummy had,' she nodded. 'And she was on Mummy's phone and I spoke to her.'

'That's nice,' Harry smiled. 'Did you know that she lives in a country called the Czech Republic?'

Amber nodded.

'That's where my mummy was born,' she said.

'That's right,' replied Harry. 'We've been speaking to Martina and she was telling us that she really wants to look after you if your mummy can't. And she'd like you to go and live with her and your Uncle Jan and your cousins Marc and Kris.'

I could see Amber's little mind trying to take it all in.

'Your aunty's going to come over here and meet you and you're going to spend some time together,' I told her. 'And if everyone is happy, then you'll be able to go and live with her.'

'Is she coming today?' she asked.

'No, not today,' Harry replied. 'In a few weeks.'

'Will I have to go on an aeroplane?' she asked.

'Yes, you'll probably get a plane to the Czech Republic as it's a very long way in a car,' I told her.

'I've never been on a plane before,' she said.

She suddenly looked really excited.

'Can I take my dollies if I live with Aunty Tina?' she asked.

'Yes, of course you can,' I told her. 'You can take your clothes and your toys and all of your special things.'

'OK,' she nodded.

Then she got up from the table.

'I'm gonna go and see the worm,' she said, running back into the garden.

'I think that went well,' said Harry.

But we both knew that talking about it and the reality of Amber having to move to a different country with a relative stranger was a different matter.

'I'll get the ball rolling with Martina and let you know,' he said.

'Keep me posted,' I replied.

In the meantime, I would keep talking about Martina with Amber to help her get used to the idea.

'Oh, I almost forgot – I got Martina to send over a photo,' he said. 'I thought it might be nice for Amber to have a picture of her.'

She had long dark hair like Amber's and a nice smile.

'Good idea,' I said, putting it on the kitchen table before I saw him out.

I was clearing up when Amber ran back in. She saw the photo on the table and she smiled.

'Oh, that's my mummy,' she gasped.

'No, that's your Aunty Martina,' I told her. 'Does she look your mummy?'

She nodded sadly.

'My mummy's got that hair,' she sighed, touching the photo.

'Will Mummy come and see Aunty Tina too?' she asked.

'I don't think so,' I told her. 'But I'm sure that when Mummy feels better, she'll talk to Harry and he'll tell her about Aunty Tina and something will be arranged.'

Social Services still hadn't been able to contact Petra and get her to engage in what had happened to her daughter.

My Brother's Secret

★

That afternoon, I took Amber to the shops.

'I thought you might like to choose a special frame to put Aunty Tina's picture in,' I told her.

We went to a gift shop and she spent ages choosing a photo frame.

'I like this one,' she said eventually, showing me one that was covered in pink and purple sparkly butterflies.

When we got back, we put the photo in it and put it next to Amber's bed. It suddenly felt like things were moving quickly. A wave of sadness washed over me as I realised, if all hopefully went well, Amber would be leaving me very soon. I was pleased for her but mentally I was starting the process of letting go.

It was a day for phone calls and information. That afternoon, Helen rang.

'I've got the phone number of the foster carer that the boys' little brother Billy is living with,' she told me.

It was a woman called Margaret.

'She is happy for you to ring her so they can have a chat to Billy.'

'Great,' I said. 'I'll tell them when they get home from school and then we'll try them later.'

'Let me know how you get on,' replied Helen. 'Is everything else OK?'

'We're all still getting to know each other,' I told her. 'I'm starting to see more of Cooper's rebellious side but it's nothing that I can't handle.'

'Great,' she said. 'And what about Keegan?'

'I don't feel like I really know him yet,' I told her. 'He's very quiet and just does his own thing.'

'Keep me posted and keep up the good work, Maggie,' she replied.

From my brief dealings with her so far, it always felt as if Helen couldn't wait to get off the phone.

As I drove to school that afternoon to pick them up, it was a relief to see both Keegan and Cooper waiting for me.

'Good day?' I asked them.

Keegan shrugged.

'It ain't never a good day at school,' sighed Copper. 'It's so f***ing boring.'

'Please watch your language, Cooper,' I told him. 'There are little ears listening.'

I gestured to Amber and he rolled his eyes.

'Cooper, I'm going to go and live in chilli pepper with my aunty,' Amber told him excitedly.

He looked totally confused.

'It's not called chilli pepper,' I smiled. 'It's called the Czech Republic. It's very exciting, isn't it, Amber?'

'I've got some other news for you too,' I said to the boys.

I told them about Helen giving me Billy's foster carer's number.

'Shall we try and call him when we get in?' I asked and they both nodded and seemed very keen.

When we arrived back, I got the boys and Amber a drink and a snack.

'I'm going to get Amber settled in front of the TV and then we can call Billy,' I told them.

My Brother's Secret

I went back into the kitchen and sat down at the table with Cooper and Keegan and dialled the number that Helen had given me.

'Hello?' said an older woman's voice after a couple of rings. I could hear a TV blaring out loudly in the background.

'Who is it?' she asked.

I explained who I was.

'Hopefully Helen told you I was going to ring?' I asked her. 'I've got Cooper and Keegan here and they'd love to speak to their brother.'

'OK,' she said. 'Wait a sec – let me go and get Billy.'

There was all sorts of noise in the background – the TV was on, there was a dog barking and I could hear some children shouting.

'Billy!' she yelled at the top of her voice. 'Come here.'

I put it on speakerphone so Cooper and Keegan could hear. They both looked apprehensive as they waited.

We seemed to be waiting ages until Margaret came back on the line.

'He's here,' she said.

I gestured to Cooper to take the phone.

'Billy,' he said tentatively. 'It's Cooper. You OK, mate?'

He didn't say anything but I could hear heavy breathing on the line.

'Billy, for God's sake speak to your brother,' I heard Margaret say.

'Hello,' said a quiet voice.

A smile broke out on Cooper's face.

'Hi, buddy,' he said. 'It's Cooper. You OK?'

'Yeah,' he said shyly.

'Keegan's here too,' Cooper told him.

'Hello, Billy,' Keegan said.

They waited for a response but he'd gone quiet again.

'Billy?' asked Cooper.

Billy let out a little laugh.

'Are you getting on OK?' Cooper asked.

'Poo poo wee wee,' Billy giggled.

Then there was a thud and we could hear Margaret shouting in the background.

'Billy, don't drop the phone like that,' she yelled. 'Stop being silly and come and talk to your brothers.'

We could hear him laughing in the background.

'Poopy poopy poopy pants,' he giggled.

Margaret came back on the line.

'He's being a silly sod,' she said. 'I think that's all you're going to get from him for now.'

'No problem,' I told her. 'That's four-year-olds for you but thanks for trying. Perhaps I could give you a call another time and we could arrange to meet up so the boys can see each other. We could go to the park or something?'

'Maybe,' she said vaguely. 'But I'm very busy.'

We said goodbye and I put the phone down. Keegan was expressionless but I could see Cooper looked devastated.

'You OK, lovey?' I asked him.

'Why didn't he want to talk to us?' he sighed. 'Has he forgotten about us?'

'Your brother's only little,' I said. 'You can't make a four-year-old talk on the phone. He was probably feeling overwhelmed and that's how he showed it by being silly.'

'Well, it don't sound like he's missing us,' replied Cooper.

'I'm sure he is. It's just hard for him to verbalise that,' I reassured him. 'I'll give Margaret another ring tomorrow and we'll try and set something up where you can meet him at the park.'

I knew it was much better to do things in person with a little one.

I really felt for Cooper. I could see he had a big heart and clearly missed his little brother. I knew I needed to do the best I could to try and reunite the three of them somehow.

SIX

Whirlwind of Destruction

As the days passed, we all started to get into more of a routine.

'How's Cooper been?' asked Louisa when she popped round with Edie one morning.

She worked four days a week as a nanny and we'd often try and meet up on her day off if we could.

'He's doing OK,' I told her. 'After all of his protests, he has started to keep in touch and let me know when he's doing something after school.'

'And what's Keegan like?' she added. 'You haven't said much about him.'

'Very obedient, very quiet,' I shrugged. 'Spends a lot of time in his room.'

He always came straight home every afternoon after school and there were no playdates or mention of any friends. I'd tried to coax him out of his room to watch telly with me and Amber or to play a game, but he always refused.

'And how are you doing?' I asked Louisa. She was constantly on my mind.

'OK,' she said. 'The nausea is a lot better and I'm able to keep a few things down now, which is good as it means I don't feel so weak.'

'Oh lovey,' I sighed.

She still looked very pale and tired.

'I've got an appointment for my scan but it's not for another couple of months,' she told me.

It was a long time to wait but I knew that would help to reassure her and help her feel that everything was going to be OK.

'You put your feet up,' I told her now. 'Why don't you try and have a little nap?'

'I can't do that,' she replied.

'Why not?' I asked. 'Edie's playing with Amber and I can watch them. I'll go and do us some lunch.'

'That would be amazing,' she smiled. 'But I'm not sure I'll nod off. I'm feeling constantly exhausted but I'm not really a napper.'

'It won't hurt to give it a try,' I smiled.

She curled up on the couch and I tucked a snuggly blanket over the top of her.

I went into the kitchen where the girls were playing and started to make us some sandwiches for lunch. When I popped my head around the living room door ten minutes later, Louisa was fast asleep.

'Bless her,' I smiled to myself.

She obviously needed it.

I gently shut the door so the girls wouldn't disturb her and went back into the kitchen. Amber and Edie were still playing happily so I started to tidy up.

I was in the middle of putting clean dishes away when my phone rang. I leapt on it as I didn't want it to wake Louisa.

My Brother's Secret

'Is that Maggie Hartley?' asked an official-sounding voice.

'Yes, it is,' I said. 'How can I help?'

The woman explained that her name was Clare Kyle and that she was Cooper's head of year at his secondary school.

'Is everything OK?' I asked.

'No, not really,' she replied. 'Cooper's walked out of school.'

'Walked out?' What do you mean?'

'He's gone,' she said. 'There was an incident in one of his classes this morning and we've just discovered that he's left the site.'

I had so many questions.

'Are you sure? Have you searched the school?'

'A couple of other pupils saw him leave while they were in class,' she said. 'So we're pretty certain he's gone.'

I checked if they'd reported it to the police and his social worker.

'Not yet,' replied Mrs Kyle. 'We wanted to check with you first just in case he'd already turned up at your house.'

'No, there's no sign of him here,' I told her.

'Can you tell me what happened please?' I asked, keen to get to the bottom of what on earth had gone on.

She told me how Cooper had been in a maths lesson.

'I don't know whether someone said something or something provoked him but the teacher asked him to stop talking and he swore at her. And when she gave him a detention and tried to get him to apologise, he stood up, flipped his desk over and walked out.'

'So what happens now?' I asked her.

'We obviously can't be having this sort of violent and aggressive behaviour so we're going to have to suspend him for two days,' Mrs Kyle told me. 'After that you'll need to come in with him to school where we'll have a reintegration meeting with the head, Mr Smith.'

I was horrified.

'Is a suspension really the right way to handle this?' I asked her. 'As I'm sure you know, over the past few days, Cooper has had to cope with a huge amount of upheaval.'

I wasn't convinced that removing him from school – the one thing that had actually been a constant in his life – was the best thing for him right now.

'We can't have this kind of behaviour in school and with all due respect, this isn't the first time Cooper's behaved like this,' replied Mrs Kyle.

I still wasn't prepared to back down.

'I think on this particular occasion he should be treated with a bit more compassion and understanding. His dad has just abandoned him and he's had to be taken into care. Surely you should take that into consideration?'

As his foster carer, I felt it was my job to fight for Cooper. I couldn't justify his behaviour but I felt the punishment was too harsh considering everything he'd been through.

To be honest, I wasn't a big fan of suspensions; some kids would actively try to get one so they didn't have to go to school.

'I understand you have to punish him in some way but what about one day's suspension or time in isolation so at least he's in school?' I asked.

'I'll have to talk to the head,' replied Mrs Kyle. 'Normally it's standard procedure and we don't deviate from that.'

'I'd appreciate that,' I told her. 'And I'm happy to talk to him and reiterate that too?'

'Please let us know if Cooper turns up,' she asked.

'Likewise,' I said.

I didn't think Cooper was going to go back to school but I didn't honestly know what he was thinking or if he was even thinking at all.

Once I'd put the phone down, I rang Becky.

'Cooper's school has just phoned to say he's walked out after an altercation with a teacher,' I told her. 'Could you let Helen know, please?'

'Yes, of course,' she said. 'Are you worried?'

'I'm trying not to be,' I said. 'My overriding feeling is he'll probably turn up here at some point as he knows his way back.'

Cooper was a streetwise fourteen-year-old and he knew the route to my house. However, I knew how vulnerable he was and I couldn't help but have a flicker of concern. Neither Cooper nor Keegan had a mobile phone – I reminded myself to chat to Helen about getting them both a basic one, as that would be something Social Services would have to decide.

I explained about the two-day suspension.

'I've had words with his head of year as my view is it's a bit harsh considering what's been going on in his personal life,' I told her.

'I agree,' replied Becky. 'And I'm happy to support you on that. I can contact the governors if you think that would help?'

I explained that I'd already said I would speak to the head-teacher about it if necessary.

'How much time do you think I should give it before I ring the police?' I asked her.

It was after midday now.

'I'd wait until six-ish if that's around the time he normally comes in,' she suggested.

It was autumn and it was dark by then; somehow things always seemed a lot more worrying once it got dark.

By the time I came off the phone, a bleary-eyed Louisa had wandered into the kitchen.

'Did you have a good nap?' I asked her. 'You were fast asleep when I looked in.'

'I can't believe it,' she said. 'Normally I can never sleep in the day.'

'You obviously needed it,' I replied.

I told her what had happened with Cooper.

'Oh no, you should have woken me,' she said. 'Are you worried?'

'I'm trying not to be,' I told her. 'At this stage, I'm choosing to believe that he'll just turn up here at some point.'

All I could do was carry on a normal.

'Come on, let's have some lunch,' I told her. 'I bet the girls are starving.'

Afterwards, Louisa and Edie headed home.

'I feel bad leaving you when Cooper's still missing,' she told me.

'It's not your problem,' I replied. 'Besides, I'm expecting him to walk through that door any minute.'

'I hope so,' she said, giving me a hug.

'Look after yourself, lovey.'

It was another long hour before there was a knock at the door. I opened it to find a sheepish-looking Cooper on the doorstep.

'The school phoned me,' I told him. 'What happened?'

He went into a tirade.

'The maths teacher was having a right go at me. She was making me look stupid and then she told me off for talking but everybody else was too. She was picking on me and I'd had enough.'

'Cooper, I can see you're frustrated but you can't go round swearing at teachers and flipping desks over,' I told him. 'You had us all worried when you walked out.'

'Sorry,' he said meekly. 'It was doing my head in.'

I told him the school were threatening to suspend him for two days.

'I'm going to call your head of year now and let her know that you're back,' I said.

'She hates me too,' he sighed before heading off upstairs.

I left him to cool off in his bedroom while I rang the school.

'He's just turned up,' I told Mrs Kyle.

'That's a relief,' she replied. 'I've spoken to the head about your concerns and on this occasion, he's agreed to a one-day suspension and then isolation for the second day.'

'Thank you,' I said. 'I think that's more appropriate.'

A little while later, I had to go and pick Keegan up from school.

'You're going to come with me and Amber to get Keegan,' I told Cooper. 'I'm not leaving you here on your own.'

He was old enough to be left in the house but I didn't want to risk him disappearing again.

Cooper sulked all the way to school and was silent in the back of the car. Even Amber chatting away to him didn't raise a smile.

'I heard what you did,' said Keegan when he got in the car.

'Shut it, loser,' he muttered.

The following day after we'd dropped Keegan at school, I made it very clear to him that he was going to have a quiet, boring day with no electronics or TV.

'Have you got any homework that you need to catch up on?' I asked him.

'You've got to be kidding me,' he huffed.

The hardest part for me was keeping Amber occupied as we couldn't go out. But we did some baking and drawing and played a game.

The following morning, Cooper had his reintegration meeting at school before his day in isolation.

I didn't think it was fair to bring Amber with us so I'd arranged for Vicky to have her for an hour or so. We had to drop her off bright and early so I could get both boys to school on time.

'Can I come in with you?' Cooper asked me as we got to Vicky's house. 'I need the loo.'

'OK,' I sighed. 'But be quick. We don't want to be late for your meeting.'

'I don't know why I need a stupid meeting anyway,' he sighed as he thundered up the stairs to the bathroom.

Amber knew Vicky, so she was fine with me leaving her at Vicky's house. Paige, the six-year-old girl who Vicky had been fostering for the past year or so was at school so Amber had Vicky's undivided attention.

'I've got some croissants if you want something to eat?' Vicky said. 'And I've got a sticker book we can do together.'

'I love stickers,' smiled Amber.

'Thank you for this,' I told Vicky. 'I'm interested to see how he interacts with the teachers but it's going to be a tricky meeting and it's not appropriate for a little one to be there.'

My Brother's Secret

As a single carer, it was good to have friends like Vicky who were DBS-checked and approved by my agency and Social Services so it meant that they could help out. I had done the same for her over the years.

I glanced at my watch.

'Come on Cooper,' I shouted up the stairs. 'We're going to be late.'

He'd been ages in the toilet.

A few minutes later, he finally came down.

'Good luck,' Vicky said to me quietly. 'I hope it goes OK.'

I could see Keegan was getting fidgety in the car.

'We're going to be late,' he said.

'Blame your brother,' I told him.

Thankfully, we pulled up to the school just in time.

Once we'd dropped Keegan off at the gates, I parked up and Cooper and I walked to the main reception.

Mrs Kyle was already waiting for us there. Cooper wouldn't even look at her as she walked us to the head's office.

Mr Smith was a tall, grey-haired man in a suit and thick glasses.

'Come in,' he said.

I introduced myself and explained that I was Cooper's foster carer.

'Do you understand why you were suspended, Cooper?' Mr Smith asked him after we'd all sat down.

He shrugged.

'I do but it ain't fair,' he sighed. 'That maths teacher's got it in for me.'

'Swearing at a teacher and pushing a desk over is not

acceptable behaviour in school,' he told him sternly. 'Neither is leaving the school premises without permission.'

Cooper rolled his eyes.

'You're going to spend today in isolation and then tomorrow you'll go back to your classes as normal and I don't want to ever see that kind of behaviour again. Do you understand?'

Cooper shrugged his shoulders before yawning and looking around the room.

'Everyone appreciates that things haven't been easy for you lately but this isn't the way to deal with it,' Mrs Kyle added.

'OK, if you say so,' he sighed.

Cooper looked bored and like he couldn't care less but at least he wasn't swearing.

Once he'd gone off to the isolation unit, I stayed and chatted to Mrs Kyle.

'This is the first time we've had a reintegration meeting with him,' she told me.

'So he's been suspended before?' I asked her.

'Oh, countless times,' she said. 'But we could never get hold of his dad. He wouldn't answer our calls or emails and then he'd just continue to send Cooper in so it was actually impossible to suspend him.'

I was shocked that Social Services hadn't told me this.

'His behaviour has been continually disruptive,' she sighed.

She described how one teacher had called him a 'whirlwind of destruction'.

'Maybe this was one incident too many,' she added. 'We're actually wondering if this is the right school for Cooper.'

I suddenly felt very concerned. I had been told Cooper was a tricky child but I didn't know he had a long history of disruptive behaviour. In all honesty, I wouldn't have taken him on if I had known that there was a chance he was going to be excluded permanently from school. As a single foster carer, everything begins and ends with me. I'm on duty 24/7 and since fostering Amber, I valued the time I had during the day when any older children were at school because it gave me the time and the space to look after her and do all of the extra jobs that come with fostering. What people often don't realise about fostering is that there's a lot more that needs to be done apart from looking after children. There's all the training you need to do, the meetings you have to attend and the recordings you have to do every day – you have to detail everything from the times and amounts of painkillers or medicine you might give a child, to writing down your version of any incidents like the ones there had been with Cooper over the past few days. I knew that in my daily recordings, I would have to document every meeting and every single discussion or phone call, including who called and when, and what was discussed. It was very time-consuming and sometimes, if a lot of things were going on, it could take up precious hours at the end of the day.

My phone rang later that night. When I saw Vicky's number, I assumed she was ringing to see how the meeting at school had gone. When I'd been to pick Amber up earlier, we couldn't chat openly in front of her in case she was listening.

'Are you OK, Maggie?' she asked me.

'Yes, but I'm shattered,' I moaned. 'It's been a long day.'

'I bet it has,' she replied.

Then she paused.

'I don't want to add to your troubles and I don't really know how to say this but—'

'Say what?' I interrupted.

'One of my rings is missing,' she told me. 'You know the gold one with a diamond that my mum got me for my fortieth birthday?'

'Yes, I know the one. It's your favourite.'

'I've turned the house upside down looking for it but I know it was on my bedside table this morning in a little trinket dish.'

'I can ask Amber if she's seen it?' I suggested. 'She likes sparkly things but I don't think she would have gone wandering into your bedroom though.'

'I wasn't thinking of Amber,' she said. 'I was with her the entire time that she was here.'

'So what were you thinking then?' I asked, puzzled.

She paused again.

'Cooper,' she told me.

'But Cooper wasn't at your house?' I questioned.

'He came in and went upstairs to use the toilet, remember?'

I had a sick feeling in my stomach as I recalled how long he'd been and how I'd had to call up for him to come down.

My heart sank.

Would Cooper really do that and sink so low as to steal from one of my best friends?

SEVEN

Confessions

'I'm sorry to accuse him but I can't think of any other explanation,' Vicky continued.

'No, I'm glad you said something,' I told her. 'I know how much you love that ring. Leave it with me and I'll ask Cooper about it when he gets home from school.'

'I'll feel awful if I've made a mistake,' Vicky said.

'Vicky, we've known each other long enough that you're never going to offend me,' I told her. 'I hope it does turn up or that there's a perfectly reasonable explanation.'

I felt so deflated as I came off the phone. After everything that had happened at school with Cooper this week, this was just another thing to deal with.

There was no point in searching his room as we'd gone straight to school from Vicky's house. The only thing I could do was confront him when he got home.

I wasn't going to say anything in front of Amber or Keegan so I didn't mention anything in the car on the drive back from school. I waited until Cooper had gone upstairs and then I followed him up.

I knocked on his bedroom door and popped my head round.

'Are you OK to have a quick word?' I asked him.

'Yeah,' he grunted.

'How did your day go?'

'Boring,' he replied. 'I didn't do nothing cos I was in isolation.'

'Make sure you bring your packed lunchbox downstairs so I can wash it,' I reminded him. 'Otherwise, it will go all mouldy in your bag.'

I paused.

'Vicky phoned me this afternoon,' I told him. 'She said that one of her favourite rings was missing.'

As I was talking, Cooper started rummaging through his school bag.

'She's looked all over the house for it and she can't find it so I said I'd double check with you just in case you'd seen it this morning,' I continued.

'You didn't accidentally take it when you went to the toilet, did you?'

Even though he wasn't making eye contact with me, I could see Cooper's cheeks burn bright red.

'Because if you accidentally did take it then it needs to be returned,' I told him.

'I didn't even go into her bedroom!' he blurted out.

My heart sank. I hadn't told him which room it had gone missing from. His reaction had told me everything I needed to know and he knew it too.

'I didn't mean it,' he mumbled, still not making eye contact with me. 'I was looking at it when I went to the toilet and then you called me and I panicked and I just put it in my bag. I didn't think, I was just messing.'

I had a sinking feeling in my stomach.

My Brother's Secret

'Cooper, when you go to someone's house you don't go rummaging in their bedrooms without their permission and you certainly don't take their things. That's stealing. I'll give Vicky a call and we'll have to go and return it to her.'

Cooper suddenly looked horrified.

'I'll give it to you,' he said suddenly. 'It's in my bag. You can give it back to her.'

I shook my head.

'No, Cooper, you need to come with me to see Vicky and apologise to her yourself.'

He clearly wasn't happy about that.

I went back downstairs to find my phone to message Vicky. While I was there, Cooper came down with his lunchbox and put it on the side. On top of it was Vicky's ring.

'Thank you,' I said. 'I'll keep it safe.'

I texted Vicky.

I've got your ring – Cooper did take it. Are you in tomorrow afternoon so he can come round and apologise?

She replied straight away.

So glad it's turned up. Hope he's OK. Tomorrow's fine x

I didn't want to drag the others to Vicky's with us so I arranged for Louisa to come round the following afternoon after school for an hour.

Cooper hardly said a word over dinner. Afterwards, I asked him to help me dry the dishes as I thought it would give us a chance to have another chat. I handed him a tea towel and he took it reluctantly.

'Cooper, at the end of the day, I don't want to have to lock things up in my own home,' I told him. 'So please think about your actions and don't break my trust again.'

'I told you, it was just an accident,' he sighed.

'You stole from one of my best friends,' I replied. 'If anything ever goes missing again, I'm going to be coming to you first.' I knew I was being blunt and very direct with Cooper but he'd overstepped the mark and he needed to know that. I needed him to understand the seriousness of his actions and that they had consequences. Stealing was something that I could never condone or tolerate, especially stealing from someone like Vicky who was part of my support system and was like family to me.

That night, I made a note in my daily recordings about what had happened. When I finally went upstairs to bed, I found myself taking my handbag with me. I hated it when foster children stole things because it meant that, even in my own home, which was supposed to be my safe space, I had to be constantly aware of where I was putting my handbag and be conscious of not leaving my purse or any other valuables lying around. Sadly, over the years, I'd fostered several children that had stolen from me. I remember going to the garage to get petrol and the shock I felt at realising I had no money or cards to pay for it because the teenage boy I'd been fostering at the time had taken them all. With the worst cases, I'd been forced to put a lock on my bedroom door and the rooms downstairs to restrict where the child had access to. I felt like a prison warden every night when I had to go round and do what I called 'lock up'. It's not nice having to live like that in your own home. You can never relax. As a foster carer, it's my job to give children a sense of safety but I also want that for myself. Just because you're a carer shouldn't mean that you lose that right and it's a hard part of the job.

My Brother's Secret

★

The following day, I could tell Cooper was dreading going to Vicky's. On the drive over that afternoon, he was deadly quiet.

'Do I really have to do this?' he sighed as we pulled up outside Vicky's semi. 'Can't you give it back to her?'

'It's the very least you can do,' I told him, handing him the ring. 'You're very lucky that Vicky didn't report you to the police for stealing.'

He stared at the ground as I knocked on the door.

When Vicky opened it, he wouldn't make eye contact with her.

'Come in,' she smiled. 'Hi, Cooper.'

'Hi,' he muttered.

'Cooper, what have you got to say to Vicky?' I prompted him.

'I'm sorry for taking your ring,' he muttered. 'It was an accident and I didn't mean it.'

He rummaged in his pocket for it. As he handed it back to her, I noticed his hands were shaking.

'I appreciate you telling the truth, Cooper, and I'm glad I've got my ring back as it's really precious to me,' she told him.

'Sorry,' he sighed and I could see he was close to tears.

We didn't stay for a chat or a cup of tea. I could see Cooper was keen to get out of there and I didn't want to leave the others with Louisa for too long as I knew she was tired.

'I know that was really uncomfortable for you, but thank you for doing that,' I said as we got into the car.

I was proud of him. He hadn't liked it but he'd gone in and apologised to Vicky when he could have kicked up a fuss and flat-out refused.

'All OK?' Louisa asked me quietly as we walked in. I'd told her in confidence what had happened.

'Yep,' I nodded. 'I'm hoping he's learnt his lesson now.'

Thankfully, the next few days passed without incident. I didn't hear anything more from school about Cooper and I hoped that his behaviour had started to settle down.

One morning, Helen sent me a message.

He's probably told you already but I realised when I glanced at the files the other day that it's Keegan's 12th birthday next week.

I remembered noting it when I'd first looked at the forms I'd been given when the boys came into my care. But with all the issues around Cooper, it had completely slipped my mind.

Thanks for the reminder, I messaged back. *He hasn't said a word.*

I would be absolutely mortified if I'd missed a child's birthday.

All my focus had been on Cooper and his behaviour and I felt I hadn't really got to know Keegan yet. And what I did know concerned me a little bit.

'Why are you worried about him?' asked Louisa when she was round one day.

School had said he was doing well academically and was focused and behaved in class.

'He's so quiet and insular,' I said.

He never did anything with friends; he spent most of his time in his room or playing on his console.

'He's never even mentioned any mates,' I sighed.

It made me even more determined to do something nice for Keegan's birthday.

'It's your birthday soon – any idea of what you might like to do?' I asked him that weekend.

He just shrugged.

'Dunno,' he said.

'Would you like to invite a friend round for tea?' I added.

Cooper burst out laughing.

'I told you, he ain't got no friends,' he scoffed.

'Cooper, please be nice to your brother,' I told him sternly.

Then that evening, I had a brilliant idea. With everything going on, we still hadn't arranged to meet up with their little brother Billy. Keegan's birthday fell on a Saturday so I thought I'd contact Billy's foster carer, Margaret, to see if I could organise something.

I gave her a call the following day when the boys were at school.

'It's Keegan's birthday so I thought I could organise for the boys to meet up,' I told her. 'I was thinking about a picnic in the local park.'

'Oh, that's a long way from me,' she tutted when I told her where I lived. 'And I've got two other little ones to think about.'

'I wanted to make Keegan's birthday special for him so I'd really appreciate it if you could make it work,' I replied. 'He's been desperate to see his little brother.'

'I'll see what I can do,' she replied.

I really hoped that she'd make the effort.

On Keegan's birthday, I led him downstairs to the kitchen. I'd blown up some balloons and there was a little pile of presents on the table and some cards from Helen, Vicky, Louisa, Amber and Cooper. Becky and my agency had sent him a card too and a voucher.

'Wow,' he gasped, as he opened the games that I'd bought him for his console.

There were also some books and a new T-shirt and some sweets.

'I wrapped them sweeties,' Amber told him proudly.

He seemed genuinely shocked.

'I thought I'd make pancakes for your birthday breakfast,' I told him. 'Do you like pancakes?'

He nodded.

'Our mum always used to make us those,' he replied sadly.

'Shut up, Keegan,' said Cooper.

It was the first time either of them had mentioned their mum and I was keen to encourage them to talk about her.

'What would your mum put on your pancakes?' I asked him. 'Do you like chocolate spread or how about some lemon and sugar?'

'Mum used to give us Golden Syrup,' he told me. 'And it made our mouths all sticky.'

'Oh yes, I've got some of that in my cupboard,' I smiled. 'Birthday pancakes with sticky syrup coming up.'

After breakfast, I told them they both needed to go and get dressed.

'We're going to meet your little brother and have a picnic in the park.'

They both looked shocked.

'We're really gonna see Billy?' asked Cooper.

'I told you I'd arrange it,' I replied.

I just hoped Margaret kept to her word and they turned up. It was a relief when ten minutes after we got to the park, I heard a car beep. Margaret pulled up with what seemed like a car full of kids. A little boy who I assumed was Billy climbed out of the back.

I could see the family resemblance as soon as I saw him. He had the same dark hair and blue eyes as his brothers.

I'd hoped Maragret would have taken the hint and at least got Billy to bring a little present or even make a card for Keegan but I could see he'd come with nothing.

However, it didn't matter when I saw the boys' reaction.

'Billy!' shouted Cooper and Billy ran straight over to them, beaming.

Margaret hadn't even got out of the car yet.

'Thanks for bringing him,' I said, leaning through the car window. 'He looks happy to see his brothers. I'm fine for you to leave him here if you're busy and you're comfortable with that?' I suggested.

As a fellow foster carer, Margaret knew that I was fully checked.

'Oh great,' she said. 'That's fine by me.'

'I'll text you when we're getting ready to leave,' I told her.

A few moments later, she wound up the window and sped off.

Billy was a sweet little thing and seemed delighted to see his brothers.

I'd brought a football with us so soon they were having a kick about and Amber had joined in too.

While they played, I set up a picnic on one of the wooden tables nearby. It was a chilly day but everyone was wrapped up. I put out some sandwiches, crisps and sausage rolls.

After half an hour, I could tell they were all getting a bit cold.

'Come and get some lunch,' I shouted.

While they all tucked in, I poured them all a hot chocolate from a flask I'd brought along.

Keegan's eyes nearly popped out of his head when I got out a chocolate caterpillar cake.

'It's not a proper birthday without a cake,' I smiled.

I'd put twelve candles in the top but every time I tried to light them, the wind blew them out.

I'd finally got them all lit when there was a huge gust of wind. Billy giggled as all the candles blew out and I was back to square one.

He had a really infectious laugh and soon the boys and Amber were laughing too.

'You'll have to pretend to blow out the candles, Keegan,' I told him and that set them all off again.

After the ups and downs of their first few weeks, it was a lovely couple of hours. I could see how much the older boys were enjoying being with their little brother again.

I hoped Keegan had had a nice day. Finally, I hoped I could get to know him a bit better and he would start to come out of his shell.

EIGHT

Introductions

Amber and I sat in the car.

'Where are the boys?' she asked me, gazing out of the window.

'I don't honestly know, flower,' I told her.

We were parked up in the street next to Cooper and Keegan's school waiting to pick them up as usual. However, we'd been here nearly fifteen minutes now and there was no sign of either of them.

I didn't want to go into the school and leave the car and then risk them turning up. So instead I called the office and thankfully someone answered.

'I don't know about Keegan but Cooper's in detention,' said the receptionist. 'You've probably had an email about it.'

My heart sank.

'What did he do?' I asked her.

'I'm afraid he swore at a teacher,' she told me.

I knew there was no point in leaving. Amber and I just had to sit it out until Cooper and hopefully Keegan appeared.

Luckily, I'd brought some snacks and I put some music on and we played I Spy.

Around forty-five minutes later, a shamefaced Cooper came sauntering towards the car.

'That woman on reception told me you was waiting,' he said.

'Cooper, what happened?' I asked him.

'I didn't do nothing wrong,' he sighed. 'That science teacher hates me. I was messing about and she didn't even give me a warning; she just sent me out and gave me a detention.'

I was starting to realise it was always someone else's fault and Cooper never took responsibility for this own actions.

'Cooper, this behaviour has got to stop,' I told him. 'School isn't going to give you many more chances.'

He scowled.

I wasn't going to discuss it any further in front of Amber.

'Also, where on earth is your brother?' I asked him.

I was getting worried about Keegan as he was always there waiting for me after school.

'He said he was going to go to chess club after school and he'd get the bus back,' he said.

'Oh,' I replied, surprised.

'It's OK, I've told him which ones to catch,' said Cooper.

It wasn't ideal as I would have preferred that he'd checked with me first but he was twelve now and I had to allow him a little bit of freedom. Besides, I was glad Keegan was doing something sociable instead of being stuck in his bedroom.

As we were walking through the front door, my phone was ringing. I just had time to put my bag down and answer it. It was Harry, Amber's social worker.

My Brother's Secret

'I'm calling with some good news,' he told me.

'I could do with some good news right now,' I replied.

'Amber's aunt Martina is coming over from the Czech Republic next week.'

'Wow,' I gasped. 'That feels like it's come around really quickly.'

'We've been talking to her regularly and she's keen to meet Amber as soon as she can,' he replied.

He explained that she'd be arriving on Thursday evening and was booked into a hotel in the centre of town.

'Is it OK if I bring her round on the Friday to meet Amber?' he asked.

He explained that the plan was for Martina to spend a few hours with Amber every day, which would increase as the week went on. Then, if Amber was comfortable, she would spend some time with her aunt at the hotel and sleep there overnight once or twice.

'The aim, if all has gone well, is for Martina to take her back to the Czech Republic to live the following weekend,' he added.

It would be under a kinship care fostering agreement where a friend or relative cares for a child.

I'd enjoyed having Amber living with me and I knew I needed to use this time to gently let go.

The process of transferring any child over to a new carer was always fairly quick. Some foster carers objected to this and preferred it to happen slowly over several weeks. All children are different but even with adoptions, as long as there were no special circumstances, I personally felt that anything that took more than two weeks was too long. In my own experience, I had seen how difficult it becomes for the child to live between two carers with their own different sets of rules.

I also believed that it became harder for them to attach when there were two lots of people around.

As I put the phone the down, I was already praying that Cooper would stay out of trouble over the next couple of weeks so I could focus on Amber.

I'd known this was going to happen so I'd already tried to start preparing Amber to go and live with her aunt and her family in the Czech Republic. We'd been looking at her aunt's photo and talking about her. At this stage I couldn't answer many of Amber's questions but they were things that she could ask Martina when she met her.

Before I could break the news to Amber, Keegan finally arrived home from school.

'Are you OK?' I asked him. 'I was worried. You should have told me you were going to chess club. How was it?' I added.

'Oh fine,' he said, not making eye contact with me. 'I might go again this week.'

'That's good,' I smiled. 'I'm glad you enjoyed it.'

While one brother was going off the rails, at least the other one appeared to be doing well.

With both Cooper and Keegan upstairs in their bedroom, I knew it was the ideal time to talk to Amber about her aunt.

She was busy playing with some cars in the kitchen. I let her carry on as I felt it was often best to break important news to young children while they were doing something else. I knew if I'd sat Amber down at the table and tried to talk to her, she would have been fidgety and not taken any of it in.

'That was your social worker Harry on the phone,' I told her. 'He's going to come over and see you on Friday and guess what?'

Amber paused and looked up at me.

'He's going to bring your Aunty Tina round to see you.'

She suddenly put down the truck she was playing with and a look of excitement spread across her face.

'Is she coming to my house?' she asked.

'Yes, she's coming here, to this house, on Friday,' I nodded. 'Isn't that exciting? That's only in three more sleeps.'

Amber jumped up.

'I need to get a case and put my dollies in and my jamas,' she told me.

'Don't worry, you're not leaving straight away,' I reassured her. 'We've got plenty of time to pack your things. Aunty Tina's going to come here and spend some time with you first so you can get to know each other.'

I could see Amber's little mind ticking over as she tried to take it all in.

'Am I going in a plane in the sky?' she asked.

'Yes, when you go back to the Czech Republic to live with Aunty Tina, you'll go in a plane,' I nodded. 'But she's going to spend a week with you here first.'

I quickly came up with a plan.

'How about tomorrow, before we go and get the boys from school, we pop to the shops and you can choose a special suitcase to put your things in?'

Amber nodded eagerly.

'Can I have a blue one?' she asked.

'I'm sure we can find a blue suitcase just for you,' I smiled.

She seemed to be filled with genuine excitement rather than worry at this stage, which was typical for a child her age.

'Is it definitely going to happen?' Louisa asked me on the phone that night when I rang her for a catch-up.

'It's pretty much a done deal,' I replied. 'It would take something pretty catastrophic and serious to stop it happening.'

'Edie's going to be really sad to lose her little friend,' sighed Louisa.

The Czech social services had carried out all of their checks, including home visits with Martina and her husband Jan, and Social Services here had applied for a passport for Amber.

That night I spoke to Keegan and Cooper about what was happening. It was important that I kept them in the loop as they were part of my household too.

'Amber is going to go and live with her aunty in the Czech Republic,' I explained. 'So her aunty is coming over here for a week to see Amber so they can get to know each other. I just wanted to let you know as you'll probably see her at the house a lot.'

Cooper shrugged and Keegan didn't say a word.

As I'd promised, the following day I took Amber to a department store in town and she chose a metallic blue suitcase.

'I want two,' she told me. 'I've got lots of dollies.'

'You're not allowed to take more than one big case on the plane, flower,' I replied. 'So we're going to have to choose your very favourite things to go with you.'

'But what about my dollies?' she asked, worried.

'We'll make sure there's plenty of room for them,' I smiled.

Amber didn't have a huge amount of clothes and I would get her to leave behind anything that was getting too small for her; I could pass them on to some of the other foster carers I knew. Hand-me-downs were always appreciated in fostering circles.

'Will there be snow where Aunty Tina lives?' she asked me.

'I honestly don't know,' I told her. 'But it's something you can ask your aunt when you see her and I'm sure she'll take you shopping when you get to the Czech Republic if you need more warm clothes.'

As the days went by, Amber was getting more and more excited.

Every morning, she'd wake up and ask me, 'Is it today?' and I'd shake my head.

But finally, the day to meet her aunt arrived.

'When we get back from taking Cooper and Keegan to school, Harry's going to bring Aunty Tina round,' I told her.

She looked like she was going to combust with excitement. By the time the knock on the door came, she'd lined all of her favourite dolls up on the sofa in the kitchen and had insisted on changing her outfit three times.

'Does Aunty Tina like princess dresses?' she'd asked me.

'I don't know, sweetie,' I'd told her. 'I think she's going to be happy to see you whatever you're wearing.'

She'd finally settled on jeans and a fluffy pink sweatshirt with a cat on it.

But as I went to open the door, she suddenly looked terrified and hid behind my legs.

Stood next to Harry was Tina. She looked to be in her late thirties with long dark glossy hair and a kind smile.

'Maggie, this is Martina,' Harry told me.

'Please call me Tina,' she smiled. 'Thank you for having me.'

She had a strong Czech accent but her English was good.

'Amber, are you going to say hello to your aunt?' I asked her, trying to prise her off my leg that she was clinging to like a limpet.

Tina crouched down so she could make eye contact with her.

'Hi, Amber,' she smiled. 'Oh, you've got jeans on like me and I love your jumper.'

Amber poked her head around my legs and gave her a shy smile.

'Why don't we all go through to the kitchen and have a coffee?' I suggested.

Amber stayed firmly glued to my side, sneaking the odd look at her aunt.

'Look at all these dolls,' gasped Tina as we walked into the kitchen.

'They're your favourites aren't they, Amber?' I said gently. 'While I'm making the coffee, why don't you tell your aunty what all their names are?'

'I'd like that very much,' smiled Tina encouragingly.

Slowly, Amber untangled herself from me and went over to the sofa.

Tina sat down on the floor next to her and started asking her questions.

'She seems lovely,' I said to Harry in a low voice.

He nodded in agreement.

'Oh no, I forgot Misty,' declared Amber.

'Oh dear,' I said. 'Misty's one of your favourite dolls. I think she's in your bedroom – why don't you run upstairs and get her?'

'OK,' she nodded, before running off.

I went over to Tina and handed her a coffee.

'Thank you,' she smiled.

'How are you doing?' I asked her.

'OK,' she nodded. 'I was very nervous about today.'

'You needn't have been,' I replied. 'Amber's really taken to you.'

'She's gorgeous,' she nodded. 'She looks a lot like my sister. I wasn't prepared for that.'

I could see she was getting emotional.

'I can definitely see the family resemblance between the two of you as well,' I replied.

'I just want her to like me,' she shrugged.

'I'm sure she will,' I reassured her. 'You've got a whole week to get to know each other.'

Amber still hadn't come back down so I told Tina how she'd changed since she'd been with me.

'She's really come out of her shell,' nodded Harry. 'And she seems very excited about coming to live with you.'

'I hope so,' she said. 'I want to do the right thing by her. She's family. My sister's let her down so badly, it breaks my heart.'

Before we had time to talk any more, Amber came in carrying two of her dolls.

'This is Misty and I forgot Julie too,' she told her.

'Wow, you've got so many lovely dolls,' Tina smiled.

I turned my back on them to pour Harry a cup of tea.

The next time I looked around, Amber was sitting on Tina's lap.

'You look like my mummy,' she said, stroking Tina's long dark hair.

'Do I?' smiled Tina. 'Your mummy is very pretty. I think you've got your mummy's hair too.'

Amber grinned.

'And you sound like Mummy too,' she added.

'That's because we both grew up in the Czech Republic and Mummy spent lots of years there before she came to the UK so she still has her accent,' she told her.

Amber nodded and gave her a little smile.

Harry and I chatted among ourselves while Tina and Amber played with the dolls.

After half an hour, Harry got up to go.

'Apologies but I have to head back to the office now,' he announced. 'Martina, Maggie will make sure that she points you in the right direction of your hotel.'

'Thanks for everything,' she said to him.

I showed Harry out.

'It seems to be going really well so far,' he said.

'It really does,' I nodded. 'She's a nice woman.'

'Even so, I don't think she should stay much longer than another hour or so at the most,' he told me.

'No problem,' I replied.

I completely understood and agreed. Even if it was going well, first visits should never be any more than two hours at the very most, otherwise it was too overwhelming for a child, especially a young child like Amber.

Once Harry had gone, I suggested that Tina and Amber had a game of *Hungry Hippos*.

'That's my favourite,' smiled Amber.

While they played, I hovered around the kitchen, tidying up and folding washing. Even though they were getting on well, it was still the first time they'd met and I needed to be around to make sure Amber was OK.

Just before lunch, I knew it was time for Tina to go. I could see Amber was getting tired.

My Brother's Secret

'Aunty Tina's going to go back to her hotel soon,' I told her. 'But hopefully she'll come back tomorrow and see you.'

'I'd love to,' she smiled.

'Can I come and see your hotel?' Amber asked her shyly.

'Sure you can, sweetheart, but probably later next week,' Tina told her and I nodded.

'Aunty Tina's going to come here again tomorrow but you can go to her hotel next week and have a sleepover if you'd like that?'

Amber nodded enthusiastically.

'It's only a small room but it's got two beds – one for you and one for me – and it's near a McDonalds,' Tina told her. 'We could go there for a burger if you'd like?'

Amber scrunched up her face.

'I don't like burgers but I like chicken nuggets,' she told her aunt.

'We'll get some nuggets then,' smiled Tina.

As I showed her out, she looked tired too.

Amber was waving from the front window.

'See you tomorrow, Aunty Tina,' she shouted, her breath misting up the glass.

I could see Amber was shattered. It does often tire children out emotionally and physically when they meet a new carer.

I quickly made us some lunch, then put the TV on so she could watch a show for half an hour, just to decompress after the excitement of the morning.

I went to tidy the kitchen and when I came back ten minutes later, Amber was curled up, fast asleep on the sofa.

My heart swelled with pride at how she was coping with everything. I let her sleep as she obviously needed it. Thankfully she woke up just before we were due to leave to get the boys.

Amber couldn't wait to tell them her news.

'I saw my Aunty Tina today,' she chattered. 'She liked my dollies and I'm going to go to her hotel for a sleepover and have chicken nuggets.'

'That's good,' nodded Cooper.

Keegan was his usual quiet self and didn't say anything.

Harry rang me later to check how the rest of Tina's visit had gone.

'Really well,' I told him. 'Let's see how the rest of the week goes but it was a good start.'

He'd already called Tina and checked in with her.

'She's really taken with Amber,' he told me. 'I could hear it in her voice.'

I was glad their first meeting had been so positive and I hoped the next few days would go as smoothly.

The following day, we'd arranged for Tina to come over after lunch. This time Harry wasn't going to be with her. That morning, Amber and I baked some cakes.

'Then when Aunty Tina comes, she can help you decorate them,' I told her.

It was always good for children and adults to have an activity to do together. It took the pressure off both of them if they were focused on a task and it was a good way for them to get to know each other.

By the time Tina had arrived, Amber had got all of the toppings out of my baking cupboard. The worktop was crammed with pots of chocolate sprinkles, icing sugar, cherries, hundreds and thousands and Jelly Tots.

'Wow,' laughed Tina. 'Somebody's got a sweet tooth!'

'I love sweeties,' grinned Amber.

Again, I was going to leave them to it but made sure I was there in the background in case either of them needed me. I got on with some housework.

'Maggie, we've done the cakes!' Amber shouted a little while later.

I went back into the kitchen.

'Oh wow,' I smiled. 'They look lovely.'

'Amber did a great job,' replied Tina.

'I think there's a bit of tasting been going on there too,' I laughed as I saw Amber's mouth covered in chocolate.

'I like the chocolate sprinkles,' she grinned sheepishly.

'Shall we get a little box so your aunt can take a couple back with her in case she's hungry later on?' I suggested.

Amber started rummaging in the cupboard.

'You choose them for me,' Tina told her.

Amber carefully selected a couple of cakes and put them in the box.

Thankfully, things continued to go well. The following day Tina came over and, this time, she stayed for lunch.

She showed Amber photos of her sons, nine-year-old Marc and Kris, eleven, and her husband Jan. She'd also taken some pictures of their house and the bedroom Amber would be sleeping in.

'Look Maggie, this is going to be my house!' she told me excitedly.

I looked at the photo of the red-brick house with the triangular roof and the clear blue sky.

'Wow, that looks like a lovely house,' I smiled.

Another day, Tina came over for the afternoon and took Amber to the park. She stayed for dinner and then helped me to put Amber to bed so she knew her routine.

'Can Aunty Tina read me a story?' she asked.

'Course she can,' I told her.

When Tina came back downstairs, I asked her if she wanted to stay for a cup of tea.

'That would be nice,' she smiled. 'I'm fed up of sitting in the hotel room alone.'

I was keen to see how she was getting on and if there was anything she specifically wanted to know about Amber.

'I'm so angry at my sister,' she sighed. 'Every day I look at Amber and think how could she neglect such a beautiful little girl? I tried to reach out and help her but by the time I realised there was a serious problem, it was too late. She won't even answer the phone to me now.'

'Addictions are tough,' I told her. 'You can't help someone if they don't want to help themselves.'

'I feel so guilty about her baby brother,' she added. 'Jan and I talked about it for ages, but I just couldn't take him as well. I feel like we're past the baby stage but my sons are so excited about Amber coming to live with us.'

'It must have been a hard choice but you have to do what's best for you and your family,' I told her. 'Baby Richard will be fine.'

Harry had told me there were several couples who were being considered to adopt him.

Tina seemed like a kind, compassionate woman.

'Do you think it's going to be OK?' she asked me. 'Does Amber seem happy to you?'

I told her how Amber had been when she'd first come to me ten weeks ago. I could see how much it upset Tina to hear how her sister had treated her.

My Brother's Secret

'She seems to be bonding really well with you,' I told her. 'I'm not saying there won't be any wobbles but so far, she seems happy and excited about moving to the Czech Republic.'

Amber and I had even started sorting through her things, deciding what she wanted to take and what she had grown out of.

On Tuesday the following week, we packed a little rucksack containing her pyjamas, toothbrush and a storybook, then I drove Amber to Tina's hotel for the sleepover.

'Have you ever been to a hotel before?' I asked her and she shook her head. She gazed around the reception area in the Travelodge in complete awe.

'Good luck,' I said to Tina as Amber ran into the room and bounced on the beds with squeals of excitement.

'Don't worry, I'm sure she'll crash out later,' smiled Tina.

'Well, you know where I am if you need me,' I replied.

It felt strangely quiet at home. Cooper was at a friend's house and Keegan was in his bedroom as usual. It felt strange not having Amber chatting along to me as I made dinner.

'When's Amber going?' asked Cooper over dinner after he'd got back.

'Her flight's on Friday,' I said.

I told them how I'd organised a little goodbye party for her. Over the past few weeks, she'd got to know Vicky and Becky quite well and especially Louisa and her little friend Edie.

'If she's going then does that mean Billy can come and live here?' asked Cooper with a mouthful of cottage pie.

It completely floored me. I hadn't even thought about that as my mind had been so preoccupied with Amber leaving.

'Would you like Billy to come and live here with us?' I asked them and both Cooper and Keegan nodded.

'If Amber ain't here no more then why can't he come?' questioned Cooper.

'It's definitely something we can think about,' I told them. 'I'll talk to Helen about it and see what she thinks.'

It wasn't something that I could promise as a foster carer. I could talk to Helen and Becky about it and give my opinion but ultimately, it was the social worker's decision. I didn't know what the long-term plan was for Billy. It could even be adoption and, at the end of the day, I didn't want to get the boys' hopes up only to end up leaving them bitterly disappointed.

NINE

One In, One Out

After that conversation with Cooper and Keegan, a seed had definitely been sewn in my mind. It was always preferable to keep a sibling group together wherever possible. And Cooper was right, with Amber leaving it *did* give me the space to take on Billy too.

I mentioned it to Helen the next time I spoke to her.

'We've got the review coming up so perhaps it's something we can explore then?' she suggested.

With everything that had been going on with Amber, I'd forgotten all about the LAC (Looked After Child) review to discuss the boys, which was scheduled for the following week. It was a meeting that happened a few weeks after a child came into the care system. Everyone involved in their care, from foster carers to professionals, such as social workers, teachers and, where necessary, the police, got together to discuss what the plan was moving forwards for that child. In some cases, birth parents were also invited along but sadly Jason still hadn't been located by Social Services.

It felt as if there was a lot going on. I wanted to make sure Amber was happy and settled and somehow it felt wrong to properly explore the possibility of Billy coming to live with us while she was still with me.

A couple of days before Amber was due to fly to the Czech Republic with Tina, I organised a little gathering at my house. I prepared a buffet of sandwiches, crisps, pizza and sausage rolls, and everyone came to say goodbye and good luck to her. I'd arranged for Tina to pop in too, so everyone could meet her.

'She seems lovely,' said Louisa as we sat on the sofa in the kitchen tucking into some pizza.

'She is,' I nodded. 'I honestly don't think it could have gone any better. Amber seems to have bonded with her right from the start.'

I looked at Amber who was happily playing with Edie at our feet.

Louisa voiced the same thought that I was having.

'Edie's really going to miss her,' she said.

'To be honest, I am too,' I replied wistfully.

Harry popped in to say his goodbyes.

'We're all on track,' I told him. 'All her stuff's pretty much sorted out and packed now.'

He told me how he'd been in touch with the Czech equivalent of Social Services and was planning on going over there in two weeks to see how Amber was getting on and to make sure that she had settled OK.

'How's the last day or so been?' he asked. 'I've been checking in regularly with Martina but how's Amber getting on?'

'She's been great,' I said. 'She's very excited about going on a plane and meeting her cousins.'

That tended to be the way with young children. They lived very much in the moment and didn't see the bigger picture.

Thursday was mine and Amber's last full day together before her flight left the following day and I'd planned for us to do all her favourite things. We went to the playgroup that she loved then we had a ham sandwich and a hot chocolate in a café, followed by a trip to the swings at the local park. But as soon as we got home, it was as if a switch had flicked and she was suddenly petulant and grumpy.

I'd made her favourite lasagne for her last dinner with me and the boys.

'Don't want this,' she told me, pushing her plate away.

'But you love my lasagne,' I told her.

'It's yuck,' she snapped.

I assumed she was tired after our busy day. After I'd cleared up the dishes, I suggested we go upstairs and run her a bath.

'Don't want a bath,' she huffed.

'You need to have a bath so you're nice and clean to go on the plane tomorrow with Aunty Tina,' I told her.

'I don't want to,' she said, stamping her feet.

Sometimes you had to pick your battles and I could see that Amber was having a wobble. Everything was a struggle and she'd turned back into the child she'd been when she'd first arrived at my house. She refused to stand still for me to help her get into her pyjamas and she wouldn't sit for a story.

'I don't like this book,' she yelled, grabbing it from my hand and throwing it on the floor.

'But *The Gruffalo* is one of your favourites,' I said.

'No, it's not, I hate it,' she shouted, her bottom lip trembling.

I could see she was close to tears. Eventually I managed to get her into her pyjamas and into bed. Her room looked so bare without all of her things in it and her new blue suitcase was all packed and ready to close up in the morning.

Finally, she seemed to be calming down.

I sat on Amber's bed and stroked her hair.

'I won't sleep in this bed ever again, will I?' she murmured.

'No, but you'll be sleeping in your brand-new bed in your lovely new house with your cousins,' I told her. 'We're going to miss you but Aunty Tina can't wait for you to go and live with her.'

She gave me a sleepy smile and I tucked her in.

It was normal for children to have a wobble before they left a placement and it was yet more change in Amber's life. She needed the reassurance that it was OK for her to go and that I'd still remember her.

Meanwhile, I was having my own little wobble. My heart felt heavy as I got into bed that night. Even though I knew this was the best option for Amber, it was always sad to say goodbye to a child, especially to a little one who I'd really enjoyed caring for. However hard it was, I knew when I'd started fostering that it was part of the job. It never got any easier though.

The next morning, I knew it was going to be busy, which in my opinion was always a good thing when there was an impending goodbye. It was the usual scramble getting breakfast for everyone and dropping the boys to school. I didn't think it was a good idea for me to take Amber to the airport.

I felt it was important that she left me rather than me leaving her. I was worried that if I took her to the airport and then left her, Amber might feel a sense of abandonment. Instead, Tina was coming in a taxi to collect her.

After breakfast, we quickly packed the last few things into Amber's case. Even though we'd been ruthless about what she was taking, I still needed her to sit on top of it to get the zip closed. She also had a backpack to take on the plane that was stuffed full of her favourite dolls.

Just after 11 a.m., Tina arrived. I was grateful that the taxi was waiting outside as it meant we couldn't have a long and lingering goodbye.

'Thank you for everything,' said Tina, giving me a hug. 'I'll keep in touch.'

'Message me to let me know you've landed safely,' I told her.

Then finally it was time to say goodbye to Amber.

I crouched down and gave her a big hug.

'Enjoy going on the plane,' I told her. 'Tina's going to send me some photos of you in your new house.'

'I'll wave to you from the sky,' she grinned.

'I'd better make sure I'm looking up then,' I told her.

As I watched her skipping off down the front path, hand-in-hand with her aunt, I knew this was the right thing for Amber.

I plastered a smile on my face and waved as Amber blew kisses through the window of the taxi.

I went inside and made myself a cup of tea and sat down on the sofa. I allowed myself a little moment of quiet to just sit and take a breath and recognise the sadness I felt.

Then I did what I always liked to do when a child left me. I went up to Amber's bedroom and opened all the windows and stripped the bed. Part of my process of letting go was to change the room around and give it a good clean. Somehow that helped me to start to move on after a placement had ended.

Thankfully the boys seemed unaffected by Amber leaving.

'Has she gone?' asked Cooper that night.

'Yes,' I nodded. 'She should be at her new house in the Czech Republic by now.'

I'd had a text from Tina to say the flight had gone well.

'So does that mean Billy can come and live here?' he asked.

'I promise that I'll talk to Helen about it,' I told them.

I could see it was something they both genuinely wanted so the following day I called Becky to discuss it with her.

'Now Amber's gone, the boys have been asking me about their little brother Billy coming to live with us,' I told her.

'I know you've got the room but is that something that you'd want?' she asked me.

'I do think it would help the two older boys to have Billy around,' I said. 'If Amber hadn't been with me already when they came into the care system, I would have happily taken on all three of them.'

I'd seen how they were together and Cooper especially seemed to light up when Billy was around. It was like the young boy softened them and helped to bring them out of their shells. I thought it might help calm Cooper and give him more stability as well as encourage Keegan to be more sociable.

'The only issue is his foster carer, Margaret,' I said. 'I feel very awkward about looking like I'm trying to take a child off another carer.'

My Brother's Secret

'I can chat to Margaret's supervising social worker about it and test the water?' suggested Becky. 'But ultimately, as you know, it's not her or Margaret's decision.'

That was down to Helen and Social Services. If they decided that it was in the boys' best interests to be together then that would be what happened.

'Why don't we all discuss it at the LAC review?' I suggested.

That was as good a time as any to get everyone's opinions on what was best for all three boys.

The review was being held at the main Social Services building in town a few days later – a building I'd been to many times over the years. It was a packed meeting room. There was Becky and I, Helen, Margaret and her supervising social worker, who was a very young-looking woman called Jessica. There was also Mr Smith the headteacher at Cooper and Keegan's school. Chairing the meeting was the boys' Independent Reviewing Officer (IRO), who had just been appointed. An IRO was there to make sure the children's welfare was the priority at all times and that their best interests were paramount, and they correlated all the information from the team around the child.

As soon as I saw their IRO, Harriet, we recognised each other. She was a social worker and I'd worked with her a couple of times in the past. She was in her early fifties and was very no-nonsense. I knew a few people over the years who had taken offence to her straight-talking attitude but I liked it – at least everyone knew where they stood.

'Maggie!' she smiled. 'I recognised your name on the files and was pleased to see that you're still fostering.'

'I'm still here,' I told her. 'Despite all the ups and downs, I couldn't imagine doing anything else.'

With three children, there was a lot to get through so Harriet introduced everyone at the meeting.

We talked about Cooper and Keegan first.

'As I'm sure his school would agree, Cooper's behaviour has been very challenging at times,' I told them.

Mr Smith nodded.

'Sadly, this isn't new,' he said. 'And it's something that seems to have escalated.'

We went over the recent incidents.

'We are starting to question whether our school is the right place for Cooper and his level of disruption,' Mr Smith added. 'We're going to see how things go over the next few weeks.'

'And how about Keegan?' asked Harriet.

'They're like chalk and cheese,' nodded Mr Smith. 'Keegan is no trouble. He's well behaved in class, concentrates on his work, no behavioural problems. I've spoken to his teachers and they don't have any issues with him.'

I knew I needed to give them my opinion. Cooper's behaviour left a lot to be desired but at least he wore his heart on his sleeve and you knew what he was thinking. In comparison, Keegan was a closed book.

'I do worry that he's a little too quiet,' I said. 'He's very insular and never mentions any friends. Although I was pleased to hear that he's joined the school chess club a couple of times a week,' I added.

'Oh, I didn't know we had a chess club,' replied Mr Smith. 'Must be a new thing.'

My Brother's Secret

We also discussed the fact that the boys had had an opportunity to have contact with their little brother Billy at the park.

'And how did that go?' queried Harriet.

'The boys all seemed to enjoy it. There was chocolate cake involved as it was Keegan's birthday but they genuinely had a lovely time.'

At the mention of Billy, Harriet turned to Margaret.

'And how is Billy getting on?' she asked her.

Margaret shook her head and did a sharp intake of breath.

'Billy doesn't listen,' she sighed. 'He's always questioning everything and he winds up the other kids. I find him very difficult and he's a lot of work.'

It was Helen's turn to speak.

'Actually, I could have a solution for you, Margaret,' she announced. 'I've been chatting to Maggie and she has just had a child leave and is more than happy to take on Billy so he can be with his older brothers.'

Margaret suddenly had a face like thunder.

'I didn't mean he had to leave,' she said, quickly backtracking. 'He's not that bad. I mean I'm quite fond of him really.'

I knew in my heart that she wasn't the right carer for Billy but I could see that I had annoyed her.

Harriet looked down at her notes.

'It's always favourable to place a sibling group together,' she nodded. 'And it sounds like it might benefit all of the brothers to be under the same roof.'

'As their social worker, I think it's a good idea,' agreed Helen.

'I believe it would really help Keegan and Cooper to have their little brother with them,' I added.

'Let's do it then,' said Harriet decisively. 'Let's get some introductory visits happening where Billy can go round to Maggie's. Then if all goes well, he could transfer over within four or five days? It's not fair to drag it out for any child.'

Margaret looked furious. I guessed that she was probably annoyed as well because she would lose out financially. When a child moves, there is a drop in your finances as you get an allowance for each child. Most foster carers try and have savings or money put away for times like this. If not, it was likely that Margaret would get another placement pretty quickly to replace Billy as there were always children looking for foster homes.

'B-but you can't just do that,' she stuttered. 'I think he's fine where he is.'

'I can understand that you don't want to let him go but this is about keeping a sibling group together,' explained Harriet. 'And I do feel that it's in Billy's best interests to be in a placement with his two brothers. This is a really positive step forwards and I can only thank you for the care you've shown Billy. We can iron out all the details with Maggie after this meeting,' she added.

I could see Margaret wasn't happy but Harriet pressed on. Helen spoke about Jason, the boys' dad, and how they still hadn't been able to trace him.

'Even though we haven't got hold of Dad, we can't leave these children in limbo so we need to go ahead with a care order,' Harriet decided.

It could take up to twenty-six weeks to go through the courts and meant that ultimately Social Services would have parental responsibility for the boys.

My Brother's Secret

As everyone chatted after the meeting, I could feel Margaret glaring at me from across the table. It was uncomfortable but, to be honest, I hadn't warmed to her. The way she spoke about Billy wasn't caring or affectionate and I didn't feel as if she had any firm investment in him or his future.

On the way out, I had a quiet word with Becky.

'I can see Margaret's annoyed with me and I know it's going to be awkward if I have to collect Billy from her house to bring him round for tea,' I told her. 'I don't want to create any drama or bad feeling in front of him.'

'Why don't I have a word with Helen?' suggested Becky. 'I'm sure she wouldn't mind stepping in to do that.'

Later that night I told the boys what had been decided.

'We had a meeting today and Helen's organised for Billy to come round for tea tomorrow. And, depending on how Billy's feeling and how you two are feeling, he might be able to come and live here.'

'Yes!' said Cooper. 'Why can't we go and get him now?'

'Billy hasn't lived here before and doesn't know me yet,' I told him. 'So it's all got to be done slowly in a way that works for him.'

'OK,' sighed Cooper, rolling his eyes.

I could tell Keegan was happy too as he had a big smile on his face.

It was important that I still used the word 'might' as we didn't know how it was going to go. Nothing was guaranteed in fostering and I didn't want to get the boys' hopes up. In reality, it could cause Billy too much upset and stress to move or it could take longer to settle him in.

'What's Billy's favourite tea?' I asked Cooper and Keegan.

'He likes beefburgers and chips,' nodded Keegan.

'Right, we'll have that then,' I told them.

The following night after school, Helen dropped Billy off. For once, both boys were out of their bedrooms and waiting in the front room for him to arrive.

As soon as I opened the door, Billy came running past me to see Cooper and Keegan and the three of them ran upstairs.

'I don't think I'm needed,' I smiled. 'I'll get on with tea then.'

After five minutes, I went upstairs to check on the boys. They were running around their bedroom and whacking each other with pillows.

'Careful boys, you don't want to hurt your little brother,' I told them.

But, on this occasion, I could see they were having fun and the grin on Billy's face told me he was enjoying it too.

He started bouncing up and down on the bed and giggling.

'These are my big brothers,' he told me proudly.

'I know they are, sweetheart,' I smiled. 'And they've been really excited about seeing you.'

Afterwards, they all came downstairs, red cheeked and sweaty from their pillow fights, and I got them a drink. Billy gasped when he saw my toy cupboard in the kitchen and ran over to it. He tipped out a big box of wooden track all over the floor.

'Keegan, Cooper, will you play trains with me?' he asked with big, pleading blue eyes.

I watched as the brothers worked together to build a train track that looped all the way round the kitchen. That's what I liked about fostering older and younger children at the same time: little ones enabled the older ones to play and be childish without feeling silly or embarrassed.

'Look, Maggie!' Billy yelled. 'Our track is very, very long.'

'Wow,' I replied. 'It really is, you've done so well.'

I could see from the smile on his little face that Billy was very pleased with himself.

Half an hour later, we all sat down for dinner and he tucked in enthusiastically.

'I like burgers,' he said, with his mouth full.

'I know you do, lovey,' I smiled.

'We told her they was your favourite,' added Keegan.

It was nice to see Keegan speaking up and joining in for once.

After tea, the boys watched a film together. Cooper and Billy curled up on the sofa together while Keegan sat on the other chair. My heart melted as I watched Billy cuddle into his big brother and put a little hand on his chest.

Shortly afterwards, Helen came to collect him and take him back to Margaret's.

'Aw, do I have to go?' sighed Billy as she brought him his coat.

'Would you like to come back to Maggie's house tomorrow?' she asked him and he nodded.

'Can he come and live here with us?' asked Cooper. 'Please.'

'I'm going to talk to you all about that tomorrow and see what you think,' Helen told him.

'I want to!' yelled Billy eagerly.

'Let's talk about it on the way home,' Helen told him.

She called me the next morning when the boys were all in school.

'What do you think?' I asked her.

'It seems like a no brainer,' she replied. 'Billy told me all the way home how much he wanted to come and live at your house and Cooper and Keegan have both said the same.'

'You know I'm all for it,' I told her. 'He seems like a really lovely little lad. He's a little ray of sunshine.'

'I think the only person who isn't happy is Margaret,' added Helen. 'But her supervising social worker is talking her through it.'

It was an uncomfortable situation and I would never openly criticise another carer. But in this case, I firmly believed Billy would be better off with his brothers.

Helen said she would organise everything directly with Margaret so I didn't have to get involved.

'I've told Billy that he's going to come to your house again tonight,' she explained. 'Then tomorrow I'm going to pick up his stuff from Margaret's in the day, then I'm going to collect him from school and bring him straight to your house.'

'That sounds like a plan,' I smiled. 'How did he react to that?'

'He seemed really excited,' she said.

As I put the phone down, I was suddenly struck by the fact I was going to have three boys in the house.

I hoped it would be the start of a new chapter, especially for Cooper. I prayed that having his little brother around would give him that sense of stability and mean that his behaviour started to improve. All I could do was hope that it would bring us all some much-needed calm.

TEN

Off the Rails

While the boys were at school, I set about transforming Amber's old bedroom into Billy's room. It was important to me that it looked slightly different every time there was a new child in there as it was part of moving on and having a fresh start. Many of the children who came to live with me had never had a room of their own before or if they had, they hadn't had a bed or it hadn't been comfortable. I liked to make sure children had the home comforts that most of us take for granted like freshly washed bedding, carpet on the floor so it was soft under their feet, cosy lamps and a snuggly blanket on their bed in case they got cold in the night. If they were with me for a while, I also liked to get them something with their name or initial on, like a cushion or a dressing gown, which helped to give them a sense of belonging.

The boys had told me that Billy liked outer space so I'd dug out a duvet set that I had in my cupboard that had rockets and planets on it. I always liked to put a few toys in the children's bedrooms too, so I moved a toy farm up there and some LEGO, as well as changing round a few of the books.

I showed Cooper and Keegan when they got back from school.

'But why can't he sleep in our room with us?' asked Cooper. 'There's room in the bunk bed with me.'

'He's only four and, just like Amber, he'll be going to bed a lot earlier than you and I don't want you to disturb him,' I explained.

Keegan especially spent a lot of time in his room. I wasn't concerned about it. He was quieter and more insular than Cooper and, like a lot of teenagers that I fostered, he retreated to his own space. Sometimes it was also a way that children coped with change and trauma – he needed space to process things in his own time.

That night, Helen dropped Billy off. She'd obviously had a chat to him.

'I'm coming to live here with my big brothers,' he told me proudly.

'I know you are,' I smiled. 'Helen's going to bring you here tomorrow after school and Cooper and Keegan are really happy about that.'

'Me too,' he said.

We took him upstairs and the boys showed him his bedroom.

'Is it just for me?' he asked, his eyes wide.

'It is,' I nodded. 'Have you got your own room at Margaret's house?'

He shook his head.

He told me how he shared a room with two other children called Simon and Lottie. The more he told me about Margaret's house, the more chaotic it sounded. Children were sharing bedrooms because one of the rooms was being decorated by Margaret's husband and her grandchildren seemed to stay over a lot of the time.

Margaret worked for the local authority and my agency had a rule for their carers that meant children could only share rooms with their siblings and it was also dependent on ages. Billy looked ecstatic that he was going to have a room all of his own.

'I want to live here *now*,' he laughed, bouncing up and down on the bed.

Cooper belly-flopped onto the bed next to him and he and Billy started play-fighting.

'Careful boys,' I warned but I could see they were both having fun.

Even Keegan, who stood there watching, had a slight smile on his face.

As I watched them laughing and joking about, I knew I'd made the right decision welcoming Billy into my home. I was sure the boys were going to get a lot out of having their little brother living with them again.

The next day, Helen brought Billy round. As it was his official 'move in' day, she'd taken him out of school early so we had a little bit of time for him to settle in before the boys got home. Becky was also there as she wanted to meet him and make sure I'd signed all the relevant paperwork and also run through a few admin points with Helen.

'We'd like to keep Billy at the same primary school,' Helen told me. 'Which I think works for you, Maggie?'

I nodded.

Thankfully it was close to the boys' school so it meant I could drop them off first and then take Billy.

'Margaret's sent his stuff,' she said, handing me a tatty-looking holdall.

It was marginally better than the bin bags Cooper and Keegan had first arrived with. However, when I opened it later on, it didn't feel like any care or thought had gone into packing it. His clothes were creased and smelt a bit musty and it looked like everything had just been shoved in.

It wasn't terrible, it just wasn't how I did things when a child was moving on. I thought of Amber's case and how much care I'd taken to make sure everything was washed, ironed and neatly folded. It's about showing the child that you value them and their possessions. I would never ever send a child off from my house with any of their things, even toys, in a binbag. Even a little thing like giving them their own suitcase helps to give them a sense of self-esteem. If an adult doesn't value their stuff, how are they ever going to value themselves, and know that they and their things are important?

Keegan was at chess club yet again after school but Cooper's face lit up when he saw Billy in the car when we went to pick him up.

'Hello, mate,' he smiled.

'I've come to live at your house,' Billy told him proudly.

'It's your house too now,' I reminded him.

I knew Keegan was going to be happy to see his little brother too. However, he didn't get back until 6 p.m.

'How come you're so late?' I asked him.

'One of my games went on for ages,' he muttered.

He was going to chess club two to three times a week now but I was pleased Keegan was doing something and mixing with people.

'Billy's here,' I told him. 'We've unpacked all his things.'

'OK,' he shrugged.

My Brother's Secret

Billy had been through so much change lately, I'd prepared myself for the fact that it might take him a while to settle in. I expected some tantrums or maybe some pushback. But he did everything without any fuss – he got in the bath when I asked, he got himself undressed and into his pyjamas and seemed to enjoy his bedtime story.

As I read, he nestled into me and played with the green and gold ring on my right hand.

'Do you like my ring?' I asked him.

'It's nice and shiny,' he nodded.

'My daughter Louisa bought it for my birthday a few years ago,' I told him. 'Green's my favourite colour.'

'I like green too,' he smiled.

It had been a big day for him and, by the end of the story, I could see that he was tired.

'OK, into bed now, little man,' I said.

He'd already said goodnight to Cooper and Keegan earlier.

He curled up happily in his new bed.

'Oh, look at the stars!' he gasped.

I'd stuck some glow-in-the-dark stars onto his bedroom ceiling so the room wouldn't be pitch black when I turned the light out.

'Your big brothers said you'd like those,' I smiled. 'Night night, Billy.'

'Night,' he said, snuggling down.

As I walked down the stairs, I was filled with relief that his first proper day with us had gone OK. He hadn't seemed too upset or distressed at all.

Louisa called me later on that night.

'How's it going now you're well and truly outnumbered with three boys in the house?' she asked me.

'Actually it's fine,' I told her. 'So far, Billy is an absolute delight.'
I described how sweet and affectionate he seemed.
'It's like he brings out the best in everybody,' I said.
She also asked me about Amber.
'Tina has messaged me a few times to say things have been going well but I haven't spoken to Amber yet,' I told her.

I wanted to give her the time and space to settle in and make sure she attached to her aunt and uncle before hearing from me. I also wanted to wait until Harry had been over to the Czech Republic to check how things were going.

We spent the next few days getting into a new routine with Billy in the house. With Amber gone and Billy at school like the older boys, I had my days back to myself too. I must admit, it was nice to have some breathing space to do jobs, attend meetings and training, catch up on all my admin and to sneak in the odd coffee with Louisa or Vicky, or some of my other fostering friends.

One morning, I called round to see Louisa. It was her day off, and I knew her scan was coming up soon and that she was getting very anxious.

'How are you feeling?' I asked her.

She looked a lot better.

'The sickness has nearly gone,' she told me. 'But that's made me worried that there's something wrong with the baby.'

'I'm sure it will all be fine,' I told her.

But I knew she wasn't going to feel reassured until she'd had her scan. She still didn't want to tell Edie yet so we had to be careful not to talk about the baby when she was in the room.

I was just coming out of the toilet when I heard Louisa calling me.

My Brother's Secret

'Maggie, I think your phone's ringing,' she said.

I rummaged in my bag and managed to answer it before they hung up.

It was Mrs Kyle, Cooper's head of year.

'I'm afraid you need to come up to school and collect Cooper as soon as possible,' she told me.

'Oh no,' I sighed. 'What's he done now?'

'He's been caught smoking cannabis,' she said.

'What?' I gasped.

'Mr Smith would like a word with you so he'd be grateful if you could come up to school as soon as you can.'

I was gutted. I had hoped things were on the up for Cooper but this was serious.

'I'll drive over now,' I told her.

'What is it?' Louisa asked as I hung up.

'Cooper's in trouble again at school,' I told her. 'I need to go and get him.'

'Let me know if I can do anything to help,' she told me.

'Thanks, flower,' I replied. 'Sadly, I don't think there is.'

I went out to the car before I called Helen to tell her what had happened.

'I'm going to go up to school now to collect him,' I told her.

'I'm about to go into meetings but please keep me posted,' she told me. 'Are they going to involve the police?'

'I honestly don't know yet,' I replied. 'I need to find out exactly what happened first.'

As I drove up to school, I went over things in my mind. I'd fostered children in the past who'd smoked cannabis and it was so strong and pungent, I'd always been able to smell it on their hair and clothes the minute they'd walked into the house.

Drugs were never something that I'd noticed or suspected with Cooper but had I missed the signs? Had I taken my eye off the ball, being preoccupied with Amber and now Billy?

When I got to school, I signed in at the front desk and one of the receptionists took me through to Mr Smith's office.

Slumped on a chair outside was a forlorn-looking Cooper. He jumped up when he saw me walking towards him.

'Maggie, it ain't f***ing fair. They've got it in for me.'

'Cooper, mind your language and save it for later please,' I told him. 'You're in a lot of trouble and I need to go in and speak to Mr Smith.'

'But I didn't—'

'Cooper,' I interrupted him. 'We'll talk when I come out.'

Mr Smith opened his office door.

'Sorry to drag you up here, Mrs Hartley,' he said, gesturing for me to come in.

It always annoyed me when people addressed me as 'Mrs' but I knew this wasn't the time to correct him.

He shut the door behind me and I sat down.

'Please call me Maggie,' I told him. 'So tell me, what's Cooper been up to?'

He explained that Cooper had walked out of a science lesson after having a disagreement with a teacher.

'He didn't come back so his teacher got another member of staff to go and check on him,' he told me. 'He was found in the toilets smoking a cannabis cigarette.'

'Was he on his own?' I asked and Mr Smith nodded.

'We've searched his school bag and got him to empty his pockets but there's nothing else on him as far as we're aware. I know you had concerns about suspension last time but I'm afraid my hands are tied this time,' he added. 'This is so serious that we're going to have to suspend him for three days.'

I nodded.

'Are you going to inform the police?' I asked.

'Look, we know what Cooper's been through and we've agreed that this time we won't get the police involved.'

'Thank you,' I told him. 'I appreciate that.'

It was time for Cooper to come in and Mr Smith went to fetch him.

His head was hung as he walked in.

'Cooper, what happened today is very serious,' he told him. 'You left a lesson and then you were found smoking drugs on the school premises.'

'But I—'

'Cooper, don't try and argue back – please listen to what Mr Smith is saying,' I told him firmly.

He shook his head.

'We're going to suspend you for three days,' Mr Smith continued.

'What the f**k?' Cooper yelled. 'That's not fair!'

'We've agreed that we're not going to involve the police this time as we're aware there's been a lot going on in your personal life recently but if anything like this happens again, the next time it will be an automatic expulsion.'

I could tell by the shocked look on Cooper's face that he hadn't expected that.

'Thanks for your time. I'll take Cooper home now and I'm sure his social worker will be in touch.'

As we walked to the car, neither Cooper or I said anything. But as soon as the car door closed, I turned to him.

'What's going on, Cooper?' I asked him. 'Have you been smoking weed for a while?'

'I promise you I ain't no druggie,' he told me. 'It was the first time I'd tried it. Another lad at school gave it to me. He said it would chill me out and that science teacher hates my guts and she was doing my head in and I needed to get out of there cos she's such a prick. When I went to the loo, I remembered he'd put the joint and a lighter in my pocket so I just thought what the hell? I didn't even like it. It made me feel sick and it smelt weird. Then that other teacher came in and caught me.'

I didn't know what to believe any more.

'That was a really silly decision, Cooper,' I told him. 'It's going to be permanently on your record now as well as giving school another reason not to keep you.'

'I don't care,' he huffed.

We headed home. Helen called me and I explained what had happened.

'He's been suspended for three days,' I told her. 'I couldn't really argue with them this time.'

Helen offered to help me out by going to collect Keegan and Billy from school in a couple of hours.

'That would be great,' I told her. 'Although Keegan's at an after-school club so it's just Billy.'

I had to admit that although Helen had annoyed me at first, as the weeks had passed and we'd got to know each other a bit more, I'd started to warm to her.

Billy looked confused when he got home and saw Cooper already there.

'Cooper finished school a little bit earlier today,' I explained.

When Keegan got home, he already knew.

My Brother's Secret

'I heard Cooper was caught smoking weed in the toilets,' he told me.

'Yes, unfortunately,' I replied. 'He's been suspended for three days.'

My aim over the next few days was to make things as quiet and as mundane as possible for Cooper. By the end of the first day, he'd cleared all his homework.

'You're going to have to help me do some jobs now,' I told him.

He rolled his eyes.

One of the tasks I'd got planned was to tidy up the garden for winter. While I cut the plants back, I got Cooper to sweep up the leaves and put them into bags.

The following day, he did a tip run with me.

I could see he was sulking.

'Why can't I go out?' he asked.

'Because you're suspended,' I told him. 'It's not supposed to be fun.'

That afternoon Helen rang me.

'How are things?' she asked. 'How's Cooper?'

'He's sulking a bit but he's doing OK,' I told her. 'He still swears blind that it was a one-off and he was just curious and to be honest, I do tend to believe him.'

'School rang me today,' Helen told me. 'They want me to go to a meeting before Cooper's allowed to go back to school.'

'That doesn't sound good,' I replied.

I was willing to give him the benefit of the doubt but it seemed that perhaps school wasn't.

ELEVEN

Hidden Dangers

After Cooper's three-day suspension was over, Helen and I attended a meeting at his school.

It was with Mr Smith and Mrs Kyle was also there.

'Thank you both for coming in,' he said. 'We just wanted to discuss Cooper and check we're all on the same page.'

I nodded, already suspecting where this was heading.

'We can't have any more incidents like the other day,' he told us. 'And if we do, I'm afraid we'll have no choice but to permanently exclude Cooper so you'll have to seek alternative provision for him.'

'Alternative provision' usually meant a Pupil Referral Unit, otherwise known as a PRU.

My heart sank. I didn't think a PRU was where Cooper needed to be right now. They could be tough, intimidating places and for a vulnerable teen like Cooper, it might mean his behaviour would deteriorate even more and potentially he'd end up getting involved in far more serious incidents. The only saving grace was that PRUs were oversubscribed and it often took months for a space to become available.

'I'd like to look at what we can do to try and help Cooper,' I said.

I felt like the school had written him off and were trying to wash their hands of him.

'What sort of interventions have you put in place to try and help him?' Helen asked them.

'We've never been able to get Cooper to engage and we could never get hold of his dad or get him to come in to see us,' said Mrs Kyle.

'Well, I'm here now and I'm prepared to put the work in with him,' I told them. 'I really don't think excluding him and him having to go to a PRU is the best thing for Cooper.'

I felt he needed more therapeutic work and some one-to-one time.

'We've got his PEP meeting in a few days so perhaps we can all talk about it then in more detail and discuss some ideas?' suggested Helen.

PEP stood for Pupil's Educational Plan and every child in the care system had a PEP meeting each term.

'That sounds like a good idea,' nodded Mr Smith.

Helen and I chatted outside afterwards and I told her how frustrated I felt.

'I don't honestly think that he's a bad lad,' I said. 'What he needs is some extra support rather than school saying he needs to go to an alternative provision.'

'We can talk about all of this at the PEP and suggest what we might want to be put in place for him,' agreed Helen.

Cooper had been through a lot and I believed much of his behaviour was down to that. His mum had died, his dad had walked out on him and he was living in care. The worst thing his school could do right now was to abandon him as well.

The PEP meeting, which was being held at the boys' school, was to talk about both Cooper and Keegan as they were at the same secondary. Mr Smith and Mrs Kyle were there as well as the head of pastoral care, a woman called Miss Robins, and Keegan's head of year, Mr Broome. Unsurprisingly, discussion about Cooper took up most of the meeting.

'Is there some sort of mentoring system that we could put in place for Cooper?' I asked.

I'd seen this work successfully with children in the past.

'We could look at organising a meet-and-greet for Cooper?' suggested Miss Robins.

She explained that this would be where the same teacher met Cooper at the entrance every morning. They'd check how he was doing and if he was in the right frame of mind to go to his lessons or instead, go to pastoral care.

'We'd talk to him about how he was feeling and he could stay in pastoral care until he felt ready to go to class,' Miss Robins explained.

'I think that would really help,' I nodded.

'And could we possibly organise some sessions for him with a school counsellor?' suggested Helen.

'We can definitely try to set something up,' she added.

Helen was also going to get a support worker to do some sessions with Cooper outside of school. It would just involve hanging out with him, spending some time playing football in the park or taking him out for a burger and a chat – it was like having a mentor.

'This all sounds great but it will only work if Cooper is willing to engage with us,' said Mr Smith. 'And he never has in the past.'

'All we can do is try,' replied Helen. 'And I think both the meet-and-greet teacher and the support worker need to be people that he likes and connects with, otherwise it simply won't work.'

It felt like we were taking some positive steps that could potentially really help Cooper manage his behaviour.

Then it was time to talk about Keegan.

'We don't have any issues with him,' nodded Mr Broome, Keegan's head of year. 'His teachers say he's very quiet but he concentrates in class and he's where he should be academically.'

'Are we sure they're really brothers?' joked Mr Smith.

I could see by the horrified look on Helen's face that she felt the headteacher's comment was as inappropriate as I did.

That night I had a chat to Cooper after school.

'Your behaviour at school has to improve,' I told him. 'Helen and I have suggested a few things that they're going to put in place to help you but you really have to try your best to make it work.'

'Why can't everyone just f***ing leave me alone?' he snapped.

I reminded him, as always, about his bad language but he just rolled his eyes.

'Cooper, we're all on your side,' I replied. 'Your teachers understand what a hard time you've been through. You've got a chance to turn things around here. But if you carry on as you are, you'll probably end up in a behavioural unit and, believe me, they're not great places to be.'

'I don't know why everyone keeps going on at me,' he sighed. 'My dad never said nothing.'

'Cooper, you're living in my house now and I care about you,' I replied. 'I don't want you to get permanently excluded and I don't believe that's what you want either. You've been through a hard time and you just need a little bit of help and support.'

I also had a chat with Keegan about what his teachers had said.

'Your teachers are really pleased with how much effort you're putting into your work,' I told him. 'So, well done and keep it up.'

'Ooh, who's a good boy then?' mocked Cooper.

'Shut up,' snapped Keegan.

'Boys, come on, be nice to each other,' I told them.

Later that evening I got an email from school saying they were going to start the meet-and-greet for Cooper as soon as possible. I knew Helen was also looking for a support worker. I just hoped all of this was going to have some effect and that Cooper could start to turn things around.

After the stresses of the past couple of days, I felt like I needed a change of scene. So when the boys were at school, I'd arranged to meet Vicky for lunch at a café in town. I reached for my usual gold earrings and my green and gold ring.

But as I opened the ring box, I gave a sharp intake of breath.

My ring wasn't there.

The box was empty.

In a panic, I rooted around the drawer checking to see if somehow it had fallen out somewhere. However, I knew a ring didn't easily drop out of a ring box.

I spent the next half an hour frantically checking everything. I searched every single drawer in my room, checked under the bed and under all of the furniture but I couldn't find it.

I had a sinking feeling as I remembered what had happened with Vicky's ring a few weeks ago. After all that had happened, would Cooper really steal my jewellery?

I couldn't think of any other explanation. I texted Vicky to let her know something had come up and I had to cancel, and then I started to search Cooper's room.

I rummaged through the chest of drawers and searched the wardrobe from top to bottom but there was so sign of my ring. I looked in all of the books on the shelves and under the beds.

I thought of all of the hiding places that children had used in the past. I shook all the pillowcases and duvets and felt under the fitted sheets but there was nothing.

All that was left were the mattresses. I'd fostered teenagers who'd cut a slit in a mattress and used it to hide cash, a phone or drugs. I checked Cooper's mattress on the top bunk. It was heavy trying to lift it but I patted around the sides and underneath, but I couldn't feel anything. All that was left was the mattress on the bottom bunk that nobody slept in. I pulled off the duvet and the fitted sheet, climbed on top of it and started patting around the edges.

As I checked the side nearest the wall, my hand touched on something cold and hard. It certainly wasn't a ring but there was something there.

With my heart pounding, I pulled the mattress off the bed. Much to my horror, there, taped to the side, were two knives. They were long chopping-type knives with black plastic handles and steel blades.

My Brother's Secret

They weren't knives that I recognised from my own kitchen drawers.

All thoughts of my stolen ring disappeared. What on earth was Cooper thinking?

I rang Becky and told her what had happened.

'What does he want with knives?' she asked.

'I've no idea,' I sighed. 'But it's terrifying.'

I explained to Becky that I'd told the boys about the spate of muggings around their school.

'Maybe that scared him and he wanted to carry them for protection?' she suggested.

We'd had sessions at my agency with the police and they'd come to talk to us about drugs and knives. I knew the statistics, which showed children who carried knives for protection were significantly more likely to end up having them used against themselves.

I explained how I'd found them taped to the side of the mattress.

'Are they knives from your kitchen?' Becky asked.

'No, they're not,' I told her. 'I definitely don't recognise them.'

Even so, she told me I needed to make sure all of the knives in the house were under lock and key.

'What about school?' I sighed. 'Do I have to tell them?'

We didn't know for sure that Cooper had been taking them to school and I knew it would give them even more ammunition to exclude him.

'I'll talk to Helen about it and let her decide,' replied Becky.

I also told her about the ring.

'It's the least of my worries now but it's just hurtful he would steal something precious from me.'

'Oh, Maggie, I'm sorry,' she replied. 'I hope it turns up.'

I felt so disappointed. I'd so hoped that things had turned a corner with Cooper but this was terrifying.

The first thing I did when I came off the phone was lock all my knives away, along with the two I'd found under Cooper's bed. I had a locked cupboard in my kitchen that I used for medicines and I put all of the knives in there. I'd just put the key in my pocket when my phone rang.

It was Helen.

'Becky told me what happened,' she said. 'I can't believe it, Maggie. What on earth is he thinking, having knives?'

'I don't honestly know,' I told her. 'It's such a shock. Do you think we should tell the school what I've found?'

'I don't know,' she replied. 'There's no suggestion that he's been taking them to school.'

'But what if something did happen at school and we knew he'd had knives at home?' I asked her.

I would rather be honest and transparent.

'Why don't we take a view when you've spoken to Cooper?' she suggested.

I spent the rest of the day until school pick-up time, churning things over in my mind. I put the boys' bedroom back together and put the mattress back on the bed and put the bedding back on it.

I went to collect Billy first and then drove to get Keegan and Cooper.

My heart sank when I only saw Keegan.

'Where's your brother?' I asked him.

'He said he was going to a mate's but he'll be back for dinner,' he said.

My Brother's Secret

I desperately needed to talk to him so I really hoped he would be back by then.

While Billy watched TV, I decided to mention it to Keegan. I was keen to see if he knew anything about his brother.

I went up to his bedroom.

'I wanted to talk to you about something,' I told him. 'Today I was looking for something in here and I came across two knives under Cooper's bed.'

Keegan looked shocked.

'Do you know anything about that?' I asked.

'No,' he said, shaking his head. 'He ain't said nothing to me about it. I've never seen them. What have you done with them?'

'I've locked them away so they're safe and secure,' I told him.

I was keen to push him some more.

'Is Cooper having trouble with any other pupils at school or feeling threatened by anybody?' I questioned.

'Don't think so,' he shrugged.

I didn't know what to make of it all any more.

Thankfully Cooper was home an hour after us. My heart started pounding as I heard a knock at the door.

I went to let him in. As he stepped through the doorway, he took one look at my face and obviously realised something had happened.

'What is it now?' he sighed.

'My gold and green ring has gone missing,' I told him. 'Do you know anything about it?'

'No,' he hissed. 'I ain't got it.'

I told him how I'd spent all morning looking for it.

'I searched your bedroom,' I told him.

'Why did you do that? I told you, I ain't got your ring,' he huffed.

'I didn't find it,' I added. 'But I did find something else.'

Cooper looked puzzled.

'What?' he asked.

'I found these,' I told him, holding up the two knives. 'Taped to the mattress of the bottom bunk.'

Cooper's face fell.

'Why were they there?' he asked.

'You tell me,' I replied.

'What?' he shouted. 'You think they're something to do with me?'

'Cooper, what were you thinking?' I told him. 'What are you doing with them? Where are they from? First drugs and now knives, after everything school have said to you.'

Cooper looked like he was going to explode.

'I swear on my life they ain't nothing to do with me,' he told me, his voice trembling. 'I ain't seen them before. Why would I want to hide knives?'

'That's what I've been trying to work out all afternoon, Cooper,' I said. 'I was hoping that you'd be able to tell me. Where did you get them from?'

'I can't tell you cos they're not mine,' he shouted, his voice raging with anger. 'Why won't you f***ing believe me?'

He stormed off up the stairs. I so desperately wanted to believe him but I knew that I couldn't.

TWELVE

Denial

I was upset, exhausted and cross with myself. How had I not noticed what was going on under my own roof? What had driven Cooper to want to get his hands on two knives? Was it for protection or had he got himself mixed up with the wrong crowd?

Until he was willing to talk to us, all I could do was carry on as normal as there was Keegan and Billy to think about. Cooper had stayed in his bedroom since I'd confronted him when he got home. I knew he was still in a mood with me so I was surprised when he came down to dinner.

He had an angry look on his face and didn't say a word to anyone.

'Why are you grumpy?' Billy asked him.

'Shut up, Billy,' he snapped.

'Cooper's having a bit of a hard day,' I told Billy.

'Only cos you're making things up about me,' Cooper muttered.

Dinner was awkward and it felt like everyone was treading on eggshells. Cooper slammed his cutlery around and I could tell no one dared say anything for fear of antagonising him.

After we'd eaten, he went straight back up to his room. I hoped that, in time, he would calm down and we could have a proper conversation about things.

That night, I got Billy ready for bed as usual. After his bath, I sat in the chair and read him his story. I could see him yawning as I turned the pages.

'Bed time, sleepyhead,' I smiled as I closed the book.

I was just about to tuck him in when I noticed something glinting on the rug next to his chest of drawers.

I knelt down on the floor and had a closer look.

My heart sank.

It was my ring.

'Billy, what's my ring doing in your bedroom?' I asked him, bending down to pick it up.

'I wanted to look at it,' he told me. 'Cos it's green and I like it.'

'Billy, you can't go taking things from my bedroom,' I told him. 'That ring is very precious to me. If you wanted to see it, you should have just asked me and I'd have shown it to you.'

'Sorry,' he said.

I felt guilty for accusing Cooper of taking it. But in a way I was glad that I had, otherwise I'd never have discovered the knives.

I knew I needed to apologise to him though.

I went to his bedroom and knocked on the door. Keegan was playing on his console and Cooper was lying on his bed.

'I've just found out that it was Billy who took my ring,' I told him. 'I'm so sorry that I accused you.'

'I told you it weren't me!' he replied. 'But you wouldn't believe me. '

My Brother's Secret

Keegan was watching quietly.

'Cooper, do you remember what happened at Vicky's?' I asked him. 'That's what made me think it was you. But now I know that it wasn't, so I'm apologising and I'm saying that I was wrong.'

'I wasn't lying about those stupid knives neither,' he snapped. 'Are you gonna say sorry about them?'

I chose to ignore that comment.

We didn't talk about it any more that evening, and the next morning, Cooper went off to school with the rest of the boys.

As soon as I got home from doing the school run, Helen called me.

'I decided you were right about talking to school,' she told me. 'I thought it was best that they knew what had happened so they can keep an extra eye on Cooper.'

She told me she'd had a conversation with Mr Smith.

'How did that go?' I asked.

'He said in no uncertain terms that if there was any suggestion that Cooper was bringing a knife into school or was found on the school site with a knife in his possession then he would be permanently excluded,' she told me.

I wasn't surprised.

'Mr Smith asked if you would be able to search Cooper's bag every morning,' she asked me.

I hesitated.

'I don't want to have to do that,' I replied. 'I think it would cause too much conflict with Cooper.'

'Could you do it secretly?' she asked.

'I wouldn't feel comfortable doing that regularly,' I told her. 'Couldn't school do it?'

I explained that I'd moved every knife in my house to a locked cupboard and that I'd be checking it every day.

'If one of my knives goes missing, I'll let you know and of course then I'll check Cooper's bag.'

I also told her that I was going to check his bedroom when he was at school.

'I will be being super-vigilant about it,' I added.

School, Social Services and I had to work together and hopefully Cooper would feel safe enough that he opened up to us.

Helen called me back later that afternoon.

'We've come up with a plan,' she told me. 'Cooper's meet-and-greet person is going to search his bag every morning when he comes into school.'

I thought if anyone was going to do it, that was best. Cooper's mentor was a geography teacher in his early twenties called Mr Long. I knew Cooper liked him as he had a fun, jokey manner.

However, Cooper was furious about it when he got home that evening.

'Mr Long says he gonna have to look through my bag every day and search me like I'm a criminal,' he sighed. 'It's embarrassing.'

'If the knives were nothing to do with you then you've got absolutely nothing to worry about,' I told him.

All we could do was stay vigilant and hope that Cooper eventually opened up to us about why he had those knives in the first place. Was he in trouble or involved with a gang? Or did he think he was carrying them for protection?

*

My Brother's Secret

A few days later, I had a call from Harry, Amber's social worker.

'How are you, Maggie?' he asked.

'I'm fine,' I told him. I wasn't about to share the details of what had been going on with another child's social worker.

'But more importantly, how are you and how was the Czech Republic?'

With everything going on at home, I'd completely forgotten that Harry was going over to see Tina and Amber.

'How's Amber getting on?' I asked him.

'Honestly, she's doing great,' he told me. 'She's settling really well.'

He told me that Tina and her husband Jan had really gone out of their way to make her welcome. She'd already started at a school over there.

'I think school has been a bit up and down, mainly because she only speaks English,' he said.

But he said her cousins spoke good English, as did Tina and Jan, and she'd already picked up a few words of Czech.

'She was asking me about you and the boys and she seemed keen to have a phone call with you all,' he told me. 'Would that be OK with you?'

'Absolutely,' I nodded. "I was waiting for the green light from you and Tina.'

'Tina's more than happy for her to stay in touch,' he replied.

It was a weight off my mind to know that Amber was OK and settling in well.

'I'll get Tina to message you and come up with a good time,' he told me.

He was clearly happy with the way things were going.

Amber's mum, Petra, still wasn't answering any of Social Service's calls but they'd emailed and written to her asking her to get in contact, and letting her know that Amber had recently moved placement.

Tina messaged me straight away and she arranged to call me the following evening. She put Amber on the line.

'Hi, flower,' I said cheerily. 'How are you?'

'OK,' she said shyly.

It was always tricky getting a four-year-old to chat on the phone.

'And how's your new school?' I asked.

'Good,' she told me. 'Is Edie there?'

'No, she isn't here tonight, lovey,' I told her. 'She might come for her tea with Louisa another night. But she said to say hello. She's really missing playing with you.'

Amber giggled.

I asked her about her dollies and her new bedroom and what she liked about the Czech Republic but she quickly handed the phone back to Tina.

'Thanks for talking to her,' she told me. 'She's been asking for a while if she can speak to you. But you know how it is – you give her the phone and she goes quiet.'

'That's OK,' I replied. 'It's tricky with little ones. They're so easily distracted and quickly lose interest.'

We chatted a little while longer. Tina sounded tired and I got the impression it had been harder work with Amber than she had expected.

'We've had a few ups and downs but we're getting there,' she said.

'That's to be expected,' I replied. 'Amber's been through a lot of change but I'm glad she's started to settle down.'

We said we'd keep in touch but I felt I would leave it to Tina's discretion. She knew where I was if she needed me.

I had enough going on with the children that I had with me.

Social Services had found a support worker who was going to work with Cooper. Jordan was in his early twenties and Helen said he was full of energy, loved football like Cooper and was enthusiastic.

'I think Cooper will really like him,' she told me.

Helen had told him the situation with the knives and he was going to try to win Cooper's trust and talk to him about it.

In the meantime, life carried on as normal and it was always busy with three boys around. I tried to cling on to the positives – Billy had settled in really well and was the sweetest child and Keegan seemed happy to go to school and was still going to chess club two to three times a week.

'He's obviously found his passion,' smiled Helen.

'Yes, I'm pleased,' I said. 'At least I don't have to worry about him so much any more.'

Each week day, I'd drive backwards and forwards between home and the boys' schools.

As winter was quickly approaching now, the nights were drawing in early. One afternoon, it was gloomy and pouring down and it was practically dark by 3.45 p.m.

I drove to pick Billy up first then headed to the boys' secondary school. Keegan was at chess club but Cooper had said he wanted a lift.

Perhaps due to the rain, the traffic was absolutely terrible. We crept along as the windscreen wipers battled against the downpour. Billy was singing a song to himself in the back.

I glanced at the clock.

I was going to be late for Cooper but hopefully he would wait. I hoped he wasn't getting too soaked.

We pulled up at some traffic lights and I glanced out of the window.

Looking in my wing mirror, I noticed a gang of teenagers walking up the high street towards me.

I noticed them in the gloom because they all had their hoods up and one of them was wearing a balaclava. They were the kind of gang that if I'd seen them coming when I was on my own, I'd have crossed the road to avoid them. They had a menacing air about them and they looked as if they were up to no good.

As I was waiting for the lights to change, I turned my head and I caught the gaze of one of them. He was the shortest and slightest of the group and he was the one wearing the balaclava. He had an Adidas rucksack on his back and my eyes were drawn to the familiar smiley face florescent keyring hanging off it, reflecting the glow of the street light.

Familiar clear blue eyes stared back at me. He froze, like a deer caught in headlights, and I saw a flicker of panic cross his face.

Suddenly, snapping me out of my thoughts, I heard the cars behind me beeping and I realised the lights had changed. I looked round but I could see the boy and the rest of the gang had run off down the high street.

A few seconds later, I pulled up into the usual road near school to pick up a soaking-wet Cooper.

My Brother's Secret

But my mind was elsewhere and I was completely thrown. Had I really seen what I thought I'd seen or were my eyes playing tricks on me?

All the way home, I was going over and over it.

I knew those eyes.

He'd seen me too and I'd registered his panic.

When I got home, I rang the school office straight away.

'Please let someone pick up,' I willed.

I knew the receptionists normally left around four and it was nearly half past now.

I was so relieved when someone answered.

'You just caught me heading out,' she said.

I explained to the woman who I was and she remembered me from the times I'd been in to have meetings about Cooper.

'Keegan wanted me to pick him up from chess club as the weather's so bad but can I check what time it finishes today?' I asked.

I held my breath, waiting and willing to be proved wrong.

'Chess club?' she questioned. 'Give me one minute.'

I could hear her talking to someone in the background.

'I'm sorry but we don't have a chess club,' she replied. 'There's a drama club on tonight and an art club and hockey and they all finish around now.

'Or could he have meant film club? But we definitely don't have a chess club at this school.'

She'd told me everything I needed to know.

All I could do was wait to confront him when he got home. Just before five thirty, I heard a quiet knock on the front door.

'Hi,' mumbled Keegan, his head down as I opened it.

He brushed past me and put his bag down in the hallway and was about to go upstairs.

'How was chess club?' I asked him.

'Fine,' he said without looking at me.

He put a foot on the bottom step.

'Keegan, I know you weren't at chess club,' I told him. 'I called your school and they said there wasn't one. Do you want to tell me what you've been doing after school three times a week for the past few months?'

'Nothing,' he said, starting to walk upstairs.

'Keegan, that was you I saw in the balaclava tonight, wasn't it?' I asked. 'I stopped at the traffic lights and saw you with that group. I saw your bag with the same keyring.'

'I don't know what you're on about,' he shrugged, walking up the stairs.

Out of the two older brothers, Keegan had always been the least of my worries. He was quiet, good at school, listened to his teachers. But had I got this totally wrong?

THIRTEEN

The Wrong Brother

I quickly followed Keegan upstairs and into his bedroom. Thankfully he didn't slam the door behind him.

'Keegan, please talk to me,' I urged him. 'What have you been doing when you told me you were at chess club?'

He looked at the ground.

'Just hanging around with some mates,' he shrugged.

'Why didn't you tell me that?' I asked him. 'You know I let Cooper see his friends after school.'

I'd always worried about Keegan being a loner and I would have been relieved to hear that he had some friends that he wanted to spend time with.

'I didn't say nothing cos I knew you wouldn't have let me hang around in the dark after school,' he told me.

That was probably true as he was only twelve.

'But we could have at least talked about it,' I replied. 'Are they friends from school?'

He shook his head.

'They're lads from our estate,' he continued. 'You know, where we lived with Dad.'

'And what have you been doing with these mates of yours?' I asked.

'Just hanging around,' he shrugged. 'Going to the park and the shops.'

I paused.

'And it was you I saw tonight by the traffic lights, wasn't it?'

He nodded.

'Why on earth were you wearing a balaclava?' I asked him.

'It's a cold night,' he shrugged.

It had been a cold, wet evening but a balaclava was a strange thing to wear to keep warm, especially as his coat had a hood.

'Keegan, I don't like you lying to me,' I said. 'And you've been lying to me for weeks pretending you were going to chess club. If you want to see your friends, then why don't you bring them here instead of hanging around shops or in the park?'

'Cos we live miles away,' he shrugged. 'They live near school.'

That was true but I still felt uneasy about the whole thing. Why had he been so secretive?

'OK,' I nodded. 'Like I've always said to Cooper, you're my responsibility so you need to be honest with me about where you are,' I told him. 'If you're going to meet your friends after school, you need to tell me.

'Sometimes I might say no but if you're going to a friend's house then perhaps I could come and pick you up later on?'

'I'm not a baby,' he replied. 'That will make me look stupid.'

I explained that I could arrange to meet him at a certain spot so his friends didn't have to see me.

I was starting to realise that although Keegan had been quiet, there was a lot going on beneath the surface that I hadn't been aware of. Hopefully now everything was out in the open, he wouldn't feel the need to lie to me. But there was something about that group that made me feel uneasy.

The next few days passed quietly and I hoped Keegan had got the message. There was no more mention of chess club or of seeing his friends and he came home on time every afternoon after school.

Thankfully Cooper seemed to be a bit more settled too. Mr Long still met him at the school entrance every morning to check in with him and see how he was. Much to Cooper's annoyance, Mr Long was still searching his school bag. Thankfully he hadn't had any knives on him and I hadn't found any more hidden in his bedroom either. Cooper had refused to talk to me about it since and I hoped it had just been a moment of misguided madness.

He'd also had a couple of sessions with his support worker, Jordan. He wasn't particularly enthusiastic about seeing him and complained a lot about the weekly sessions. Jordan had come and collected him and they'd played football in the park and another time, Jordan had taken him for a milkshake in the local shopping centre. So far, Cooper hadn't opened up much to him; however, it was early days and he had gone with Jordan for an hour, which felt like a win to me. I hoped that gradually, as Cooper got to know Jordan better and felt more relaxed, he might start communicating. Jordan had broached the subject of the knives with him and Cooper was still absolutely adamant that he'd had nothing to do with them.

Fortunately, Billy was still settling in well and brought me some much-needed light relief with his sweetness and affection.

Along with fostering three children came a lot of paperwork. It was still early enough in the placement to have to do daily recordings and it was a lot to write up at the end of a long day. One evening, I was coming down with a cold and I was exhausted and knew I needed to go to bed when the kids did. I quickly emailed Becky to apologise.

Not feeling too well tonight but my recordings will be with you in the morning.

I let her know there was nothing much to report and it was all mundane, day-to-day activities.

Thankfully, after an early night, I felt much better the following morning. After dropping all three boys at school, I headed home and fuelled by tea and digestive biscuits, I quickly typed out my notes from the previous day. Once I'd emailed them over to Becky, I found myself mindlessly scrolling through Facebook before I got on with some cleaning. I was a sucker for picking things up second-hand, particularly toys and furniture, and I'd bagged myself quite a few bargains over the years. I belonged to quite a few local Facebook groups and I found myself reading a post. It was from the son of a local shopkeeper of a shop I recognised, as I drove past it every day on the way to Cooper and Keegan's secondary school.

Ten days since my poor dad was held up at knifepoint in the newsagents he's run for thirty years. Somebody must know these kids. They made my elderly dad very frightened and upset – he doesn't want to go back to work now. All for the sake of some sweets, crisps and cans of fizzy drinks. Police have been useless so let's find these scumbags.

Something made me click on the grainy CCTV recording. There was no sound but I held my breath as five teenagers came into shot. Four of them had their hoods up so you couldn't

My Brother's Secret

see their faces. There was one other one – much smaller than the rest of them – who walked straight up to the counter and brazenly pulled a knife out of his pocket. He didn't have a hoodie on, but he was facing away from the camera so you could only see the back of his head. While the poor shopkeeper quivered in terror, the other hoodies cleared the shelves and shoved as much as they could into their pockets and bags.

It was all over in seconds. I was about to close the video down but something made me pause. In the closing seconds of the CCTV footage, the person who had threatened the shopkeeper with a knife turned round. I could tell from his build that he was just a boy and this time he was looking straight at the camera.

A pair of familiar eyes stared up at the camera through the holes in the balaclava that he was wearing.

As the rest of the gang came running towards him, he quickly shoved the knife into his pocket and they fled.

As the video ended and it moved on to the next one, I couldn't believe what I'd just seen.

No, I was jumping to conclusions. Surely I had got this wrong?

However, something made me watch the video again. And again. *The glint of a familiar florescent smiley face keyring.*

After I'd watched it three or four times, I knew I needed to ring Becky. My hands were shaking as I dialled her number.

'I need to talk to you,' I said, my voice quivering. 'I've seen something awful on Facebook.'

'Maggie, what is it?' she asked. 'You sound upset.'

I explained how I'd seen some distressing CCTV footage of a robbery in a shop near the boys' school and how the shopkeeper had been held up at knifepoint.

'I'm sure it's Keegan in the video,' I told her. 'I think he was the one threatening the shopkeeper with the knife.'

'No, it can't be him, Maggie,' replied Becky. 'Surely not? He doesn't strike me as the kind of kid that would threaten a shopkeeper with a knife.'

'Call it instinct but my gut is telling me that it's Keegan in that footage,' I told her firmly.

'But what makes you think that?' asked Becky.

I explained how the other night I'd seen Keegan with his mates at the traffic lights.

'As you know, he's been lying to me about going to chess club,' I told her. 'I saw him with his mates the other night. Just like in the video, all the people he was hanging around with were older and taller lads.'

'But that could apply to so many kids,' said Becky.

'And the lad in the video was shorter and he was wearing a balaclava – just like Keegan was when I saw him.'

'But anyone can get hold of a balaclava,' replied Becky.

She paused.

'Maggie, I think you've got this wrong,' she told me. 'You have no solid proof that the kid in the video with a knife is Keegan.'

At the mention of a knife, the penny suddenly dropped.

'How could I have been so stupid?' I gasped. 'I automatically assumed those knives under the bed were Cooper's. But what if they were Keegan's all along?'

I'd been so focused on Cooper and his disruptive behaviour that I hadn't really paid much attention to Keegan who, up until now, had been such a closed book.

I could tell Becky thought that I was jumping to conclusions.

My Brother's Secret

'Maggie, you can't be sure of any of this,' she told me. 'It's a feeling, you don't have any concrete proof that the person in the footage is Keegan. He's twelve years old. It can't be him.'

'It is,' I replied. 'I just know it. Please believe me. They're his eyes, he's got the same small, slight build and he's got a rucksack with an identical keyring.'

'OK,' she said, 'if you're convinced, I need to call Helen and tell her your suspicions as this is really serious.'

'I know,' I replied.

After I'd hung up the call to Becky, I watched the video over and over again. The more I watched it, the more I was convinced that I wasn't seeing things and the boy with the knife was Keegan.

Five minutes later, Helen called me.

'Becky just rang me,' she said. 'But I think she's getting mixed up. She said you thought you'd seen Keegan holding up a shop. I'm assuming she meant Cooper?'

'No, sadly she's right,' I replied. 'I think it is Keegan.'

Helen sounded as shocked as I felt.

'But why?' she asked. 'How?'

'I think I need to show you the CCTV footage in person,' I told her.

'I'll come straight round now,' she replied.

Thirty minutes later, she was sat in my kitchen. I clicked on the CCTV footage as we both sat and watched it in silence.

I could see Helen studying the screen.

'I hate to say it but I think you're right,' she sighed. 'That end part where the kid with the knife looks up at the CCTV camera . . . I know it's black and white but the eyes certainly look like Keegan's.'

'Are you going to contact the police?' I asked her.

'I think this is so serious that I have to,' she nodded. 'I need to call my manager first though, just to let her know our suspicions and get her advice.'

'OK,' I nodded. 'But what if I've got this really wrong and it's not him?'

'It's a chance we have to take,' said Helen. 'Let's hope the police can rule him out.'

I really hoped that I'd got this wrong and it wasn't Keegan.

Helen's manager agreed that she needed to pass our suspicions on to the police. I made us both a cup of tea while she went into the front room and made the call.

'The police want to come round here when Keegan gets home from school,' she told me. 'They'll want to take him down to the station and question him.'

'What, they're going to arrest him?' I asked, shocked.

'Well, I don't think they're going to put handcuffs on him and march him out to a police car, but it's a serious enough offence that they want to interview him down at the station so they can record it.'

'He'll a need a responsible adult with him too,' she added. 'The only issue is, I have an afternoon of meetings.'

'Perhaps I could go with him?' I asked her.

Normally it would be the social worker's responsibility to be with a child at times like this as they had parental responsibility. This meant the local authority made the big decisions around the child and their future. As a foster carer, I didn't have that: I only had what was called delegated authority, which meant I could make day-to-day decisions like taking them to the doctor or getting their hair cut.

'I'll have to check with my manager but I'm sure she'll agree that's OK,' she nodded. 'But what about Cooper and Billy?'

'I'll see if my friend Vicky can come round,' I told her.

I explained that she was an experienced foster carer too so she'd had all the relevant checks.

'The police stressed that we mustn't talk to Keegan about our suspicions or mention anything about the CCTV video before they come round,' Helen told me.

'But what do I do then?' I asked.

'You'll have to go and collect the boys from school as normal and then bring them back here,' Helen told me.

'It's going to be so hard pretending everything is normal and acting as if nothing has happened,' I replied.

'I know,' she nodded. 'But I'm sure you appreciate that if you alert Keegan to the fact the police are coming round then he has time to think up a story or there's even a chance he could run.'

I'd had other cases where the children I was fostering had got in trouble with the police and I knew they didn't like anyone talking to them before they had questioned them.

'The other option is for the police to go to school and pick Keegan up from there?' she suggested. 'I could ask them if they'd be prepared to do that instead?'

'No, I'd rather him be here,' I said.

It felt safer for Keegan for the police to come here. I knew how mortified he would be to be taken off by the police from school and there was even more of a risk of him running off.

'What if I've got this all wrong?' I asked Helen.

Keegan had already been through so much. What if I was putting him through more stress and upset for no reason?

'In a way, I hope you have,' said Helen.

I didn't want it to be true either. I was already angry at myself for not realising that Keegan had been lying to me for months. But this too? This felt like it could be the start of something incredibly serious.

'Good luck, Maggie,' Helen said before she left. 'Give me a call from the police station and let me know what's happening.'

'I will do,' I replied.

I knew it was going to be a long day. As the hours ticked by, I was already dreading pick-up time. It was so hard to keep a poker face and pretend nothing out of the ordinary was happening.

I also called Vicky as I needed her to come round and stay with Cooper and Billy while I went to the police station. As she was a foster carer, I knew I could tell her everything and it would remain confidential.

'I need your help,' I asked her. 'Could you come round here after you've picked Paige up from school? The police are going to be turning up and I'm going to have to go to the police station with Keegan.'

'Don't you mean Cooper?' she asked, puzzled.

Vicky sounded as shocked as I had been when I explained what had happened.

'It might not be true, of course,' I told her. 'I could have got this completely wrong and we'll be back before you know it.'

'I'm happy to help,' Vicky told me. 'What an awful situation.'

By the time it came to collect the boys from school, my stomach was churning with nerves. It was so hard to act normal when things were anything but.

My Brother's Secret

But I plastered a smile on my face, and went in and collected Billy from his primary school. He skipped back to the car, his little hand in mine, oblivious to the drama that was awaiting us all at home.

'My teacher said we're going on a school trip,' he told me. 'We're going to the woods and we're going to build a den.'

'Yes,' I nodded. 'That's exciting isn't it? I got the letter the other day in your school bag.'

'They want mummies and daddies to come but I haven't got a mummy,' he told me matter-of-factly. 'My mummy's dead.'

'Yes, I know she is, sweetheart,' I said, squeezing his hand. 'Would it be OK if I came on your trip with you?'

He smiled.

'I think I'm gonna need some wellies cos my teacher said it's muddy,' he added.

'We can sort you out a pair of those,' I told him.

As soon as we got into the car, reality hit and I had to swallow the lump in my throat as we drove to Keegan and Cooper's school and I saw them both waiting.

'Good day, boys?' I asked, trying not to sound strained.

It was so hard to try and sound upbeat. I wanted to stop the car and turn round to Keegan and ask him, 'Was that you on the CCTV footage? What on earth were you thinking?'

I also wanted to apologise to Cooper for accusing him of having the knives. I'd read the situation all wrong and I'd been so blinkered to label him 'the naughty one'. I felt it was really important when that happened to apologise to children. They needed to know that adults can get things wrong and we're only human. But I couldn't do any of that.

As soon as we got home, I was on tenterhooks, waiting for that knock on the door. Helen had told the police when we were due to arrive back from school but I wasn't sure what time they were going to turn up.

I nearly jumped out of my skin when the door went.

It was a relief to see Vicky and Paige standing there.

'I thought I'd pop in for a coffee,' she said in a loud voice.

'Oh lovely,' I told her. 'Come on in.'

I led her into the kitchen.

'All OK?' she whispered under her breath, and I nodded.

I felt better with Vicky being there for moral support. I wasn't sure how Keegan was going to react when he saw the police. He could go berserk and lash out. It hadn't been too long ago since I'd fostered a teenager called PJ, who'd thrown a chair at me when he realised I'd called the police on him and I'd ended up in hospital. He'd ended up in a secure children's home and, as far as I knew from the last I'd heard, that was where he still was now.

As the time ticked by, I nervously glanced at the clock, dreading the police's arrival.

Keegan went up to his room while Cooper was in the kitchen with Vicky and I, having a snack. Billy and Paige were happily playing in the corner.

We'd been back forty minutes when the knock at the door finally came.

I glanced at Vicky.

'Are you OK to keep everyone in here for a minute while I get the door?' I asked her.

'Absolutely,' she nodded.

My heart was pounding out of my chest as I closed the kitchen door and walked down the hallway towards the front door.

My Brother's Secret

Two male police officers were on the doorstep. They both showed me their IDs.

'I'm DC Burgess,' one of them said. 'And this is my colleague DC Fiddis. Is the young man at home?'

'He's just upstairs,' I told them. 'He doesn't know you're coming so I'm not sure how he's going to react.'

'That's OK,' one of them nodded. 'Let's get him down here and we'll see what happens.'

My head was spinning as I walked to the foot of the stairs.

'Keegan, can you come down here please?' I yelled. 'There's somebody here to see you.'

FOURTEEN

Questions

As I waited at the bottom of the stairs for Keegan to appear, so many thoughts raced through my mind. It felt like a strange predicament to be in – I was worried that I'd got this completely wrong but, at the same time, I desperately hoped that I had.

The police officers looked impatient.

'Keegan,' I called again, more firmly this time. 'Please come down here now. I need to talk to you.'

'I'm coming!' he shouted.

His face fell and he paused at the top of the stairs when he saw the two uniformed officers in the doorway.

'What's happening?' he asked. 'Why are they here?'

'Keegan, they need to talk to you in the front room for a moment,' I told him.

He suddenly looked panicked.

'But why do they need to speak to me?' he asked. 'Has something happened to my dad?'

'Don't worry, nothing's happened to your dad,' PC Burgess said. 'Come down here son and we'll explain everything to you.'

'I'll be with you too,' I reassured him.

Keegan looked terrified.

He and I sat on the sofa while the officers sat on the armchairs. They introduced themselves to him.

'I'll get straight to the point,' said DC Fiddis. 'I don't know whether you're aware, but a video has been posted online. It's CCTV footage of a robbery that took place in a shop and your name has come up as possibly being one of the people involved in that incident.'

'What?' gasped Keegan. 'That weren't even me.'

'We need to take you down to the police station, Keegan, to ask you a few questions,' added DC Fiddis.

'No,' he said. 'I'm not going nowhere. I've not done nothing.'

'Keegan, if that's the case, then all you need to do is go down to the police station and tell them that,' I urged him.

'I told you, I ain't done nothing,' he repeated. 'It ain't me.'

'Let's have a chat about it at the police station,' DC Fiddis told him. 'If it wasn't you, then we'll soon clear that up.'

Keegan suddenly looked so small and scared.

'Maggie, tell them,' he begged me. 'Tell them that I ain't done nothing.'

'Keegan, you need to do what the officers are saying,' I told him calmly. 'I'll come with you and they'll talk you through everything.'

DC Fiddis nodded.

'But why do I have to go to the police station?' he asked. 'Why can't you ask me stuff here?'

'We have to do this formally and there's a proper process that we need to follow,' DC Burgess replied. 'We need to

My Brother's Secret

ask you a few questions and take a statement and we need to record that in case it has to be used as evidence in the future.'

Keegan looked terrified.

'But I ain't done nothing. There's no evidence. You've got this all wrong.'

'That's absolutely fine. We just need you to go through this with us at the station so we can rule you out of our enquiries.'

I patted Keegan's hand.

'You wait here with the officers and I'll go and tell Vicky that we're going,' I told him.

I got up and quickly walked to the kitchen and popped my head around the door. Cooper was tucking into a sandwich and Billy was still playing with Paige.

Vicky looked at me expectantly.

'I'm just going to pop out with Keegan,' I told her. 'I don't know how long we're going to be but help yourself to some dinner. There are pizzas in the fridge and some oven chips in the freezer,' I added. 'And if it gets late, then use my bed for Paige.'

'Thanks,' she said. 'I hope it all goes alright.'

Billy looked up.

'Can I come?' he asked.

'No, flower, I just need to take Keegan somewhere,' I told him. 'You're busy playing.'

I got my bag, put on my coat and grabbed Keegan's jacket from the end of the banister. Then I went back into the living room.

'Here's your coat,' I told him, holding it out to him.

'I don't want it,' he said quietly, pushing my hand away.

'It's cold out there,' I told him.

'Just leave it,' he snapped. 'I don't want to bring it.'

I'd never seen Keegan so rattled. I could see he was stressed.

I quickly shoved it in my bag anyway. I knew police stations were sometimes old, chilly buildings and he might be glad of it later.

I followed the two DCs down the path and we got into the back of their patrol car. They told us that the station was a half an hour's drive away.

'I don't know why they think it's me,' muttered Keegan. 'I ain't got nothing to do with a robbery.'

'That's fine. Let's go down and make a statement. All you need to do is tell the truth, then hopefully they'll realise you're not involved.'

Thankfully Keegan was quiet for the rest of the journey. Meanwhile, I was feeling very stressed and going over everything again in my mind.

What if I'd got this totally wrong and it wasn't Keegan in that CCTV footage? He'd been through so much and I was putting him through more trauma. I'd never be able to forgive myself if that was the case and eventually he would know that it was me who had suspected him.

However, I knew it was too late to go back now.

The police station wasn't one that I'd been to before. It was a run-down eighties brick building off a main road. In my experience, police stations were never nice places but this one looked particularly gloomy.

It was dark outside now and it was starting to rain.

'Do you want your coat?' I asked Keegan as we got out of the car. 'It's in my bag.'

'No,' he snapped. 'I told you not to bring it.'

The two DCs led us into the reception area and took us through a door.

My Brother's Secret

'We're going to take you to one of the interview rooms,' DC Burgess told us.

It was a windowless room with a table and four blue plastic chairs and a large recording device on the table.

'Please sit down,' DC Burgess told us.

'Can I get either of you a drink of water?' he asked and we both shook our heads.

DC Fiddis explained that he was going to start recording. As the tape started rolling, he explained who everyone was in the room.

'You can ask for a break whenever you want,' he told Keegan.

'I just wanna get this over with and go home,' he sighed.

The police started asking him questions. They didn't tell him anything about the incident itself or that, to my relief, I was the one who alerted them to the fact that it looked like Keegan in the CCTV footage.

'I know this might be difficult off the top of your head but can you remember where you were after school on Tuesday the eleventh?' DC Fiddis asked him. 'It was about a week and a half ago.'

Keegan shrugged.

'Try and cast your mind back,' DC Fiddis added. 'Do you do anything on a Tuesday?'

'Oh, if it was a Tuesday then I'd be at chess club,' he replied. 'I go every Tuesday, Wednesday and Thursday after school.'

'You obviously like chess then?' asked DC Burgess and Keegan nodded.

I was there as Keegan's responsible adult and I was very much an observer in this interview process so I knew I couldn't interrupt. But I also knew that I couldn't sit there and let Keegan lie through his teeth either.

'What time do you generally get home when you've been to chess club?' DC Fiddis asked him.

'It ends at quarter to five then I have to get two buses back to Maggie's house so maybe about six?' added Keegan.

I couldn't sit there and listen to this any more.

'Do you think we could have a break soon?' I asked. 'I'm sure Keegan could do with a drink or a trip to the loo.'

As a minor, he was entitled to as many breaks as he needed.

'Yes, that's fine,' nodded DC Fiddis. 'I could do with a visit to the loo myself.'

He stopped the tape, then went out to the toilet while DC Burgess went out into the hallway to make a quick call. It gave me a few minutes on my own with Keegan.

'Keegan, what on earth are you thinking?' I asked him. 'They're going to be checking with me everything that you're saying and I can't back it up. You and I both know there never was a chess club. You need to let them know that you lied about it to me and you have to tell them where you really were that night.'

'But I dunno where I was,' he sighed. 'I can't remember. I would have been with my mates somewhere.'

'Well you need to tell them that,' I urged him. 'You have to tell them the truth. If you want them to believe you, you have to be honest from the word go.'

Just then DC Fiddis came back in followed by DC Burgess carrying a cup of water for Keegan and a tea for me.

'Is everyone ready to resume?' he asked.

I nodded and Keegan shrugged. He pressed 'record' on the tape again.

'So, Keegan, you were telling us that on Tuesday the eleventh you were at chess club?'

Keegan looked down at the floor.

'Sorry, I got stuff mixed up,' he said meekly. 'I wasn't at chess club.'

'So you didn't go to chess club that Tuesday night?' asked DC Fiddis.

Keegan shook his head.

'I made it up,' he sighed. 'There isn't a chess club. I was hanging round with my mates after school but I knew Maggie wouldn't let me, so I lied and said I was at chess club.'

'So where were you that night of the eleventh then, with your mates?' asked DC Burgess.

'Dunno' he told them. 'I don't remember. Just hanging round somewhere.'

'By "somewhere", could you have been hanging round the shops?' he asked.

'Maybe,' replied Keegan. 'But not that shop.'

'Which shop is that?' questioned DC Burgess.

'Not the one by school that got robbed,' replied Keegan.

'Keegan, how do you know that's the shop that we mean?' he asked him.

'I just heard it was that one that got robbed, that's all,' he replied. 'That don't mean that I did it.'

Keegan was getting upset now and I could see that his body was shaking.

It was freezing in the interview room so I rummaged in my bag to get his jacket. As I pulled it out and put it on my lap, I felt something in one of the inner pockets.

Something long and hard. My heart started thumping out of my chest as I looked down and carefully reached into his pocket.

I didn't even need to see the object to know what it was.

'Please could you stop the tape for a moment?' I said.

DC Burgess did as I asked.

Keegan stared at me suspiciously

'What is it?' DC Fiddis asked.

'Please could I have a quick word with you outside?' I replied.

He followed me out of the interview room into the corridor outside.

'I think I need to show you this,' I told him.

I reached into the pocket of Keegan's jacket and pulled out the knife. The blade glinted in the bright glare of the harsh lights in the corridor.

Oh Keegan, I thought to myself. What on earth have you done?

FIFTEEN

Shockwaves

My legs felt all wobbly as DC Fiddis and I walked back into the interview room. I was still in shock at the fact that Keegan had been walking around with a knife on him.

We took our seats and DC Fiddis started up the tape again.

I held my breath as I knew what was about to happen.

He placed the knife, which he'd put into a clear plastic evidence bag, on the table in front of him.

'Keegan, what can you tell me about this?' he asked.

Keegan's mouth gaped open and he turned and looked at me accusingly.

'I found it in your coat pocket,' I told him. 'I had to show it to them.'

Keegan shook his head.

'I swear it ain't mine,' he blurted out. 'I'm keeping it for a friend.'

'Keegan, is this the same knife that was used to threaten the shopkeeper in the video?' DC Fiddis asked him. 'Because if we look at the CCTV footage, we'll be able to tell if it is so we'll know if you're lying.'

This time Keegan didn't say anything. He looked panicked, like a scared little boy.

'Keegan, tell me about the knife,' urged DC Burgess. 'What on earth is a twelve-year-old boy doing walking around with a knife in his coat pocket? Where did you get it from?'

All of his earlier bravado was suddenly gone. Keegan put his head in his hands and started to cry.

'I didn't mean it,' he sobbed. 'I wasn't going to hurt nobody. My mates made me go to the shop and do it. They just wanted me to scare him so they could nick some stuff.'

'But why didn't you say no to them?' asked DC Burgess.

'They made me do it,' he wept. 'They said if I didn't then they'd use the knife on me and hurt me. I had to otherwise they were gonna stab me.'

He looked genuinely terrified as the whole sorry story came tumbling out.

'Who are these mates of yours?' asked DC Fiddis.

Keegan tearfully explained that they were older boys from his estate – fourteen and fifteen-year-olds.

'When I went to the shop sometimes after school, they'd talk to me,' he said. 'They seemed nice and they asked if I wanted to hang round with them.'

I could see how easy Keegan must have been to manipulate. Younger, vulnerable and with no friends of his own, he'd been easily impressed by these older lads.

'At first we'd hang around the park and play football after school,' he said.

He described how they'd given him sweets, crisps and cans of fizzy drinks and bought him chips.

'Then one night, they started hassling some younger kids in the park,' he explained. 'I shouted at them to stop it but one of the lads got out a knife and they took money off one and stole bags and phones. They just laughed when the kids got scared.'

'Why didn't you tell anyone what had happened?' asked DC Burgess.

'Cos they said I'd been there as well and I'd get into trouble if I told anyone. They said if I told on them, they'd cut me up.'

'You mean they'd stab you?' asked DC Fiddis, and Keegan nodded.

He described how they'd given him the knives to keep and how he'd hidden them at my house. Once again, I felt a pang of guilt for automatically blaming Cooper and I knew I owed him a big apology.

'Maggie found them and took them away and they went mad at me,' he told the officers. 'They said I owed them.'

My heart broke at the thought of him carrying this around for the past few weeks, too terrified to say anything.

'Can you give us these boys' names?' DC Fiddis asked.

Keegan shook his head.

'They'll kill me,' he muttered. 'I can't say nothing.'

'Keegan, now that you've told us all of this, we'll make sure that you're safe,' DC Burgess told him. 'But we need to speak to these boys and ask them some questions too. If things are as you've told us, if we don't stop them, they'll keep threatening people.'

'I'm not going to grass them up,' he mumbled, his hands shaking.

'Keegan, if they're carrying knives, one day they might hurt someone or someone might fight back and they'll get hurt,' DC Fiddis added. 'We don't want that to happen and we can't stop that unless we know who they are.'

Keegan paused.

'Please don't tell them it was me that told,' he snivelled.

'Keegan, we will make sure that we do everything to protect you,' DC Burgess told him.

Through his tears, he gave them the names of five boys. He only knew their first names but he told the police which flats they lived in on his old estate.

'Do they go to your school?' DC Fiddis asked but he shook his head.

I was proud of Keegan for telling the truth but I could see that he was not only very frightened, but exhausted too.

'Can I go home now?' he asked meekly.

'I'm afraid not straight away,' DC Fiddis told him. 'We might need to ask you some more questions.'

'Are you going to charge him?' I asked.

Keegan looked horrified.

'But I told you, they made me do it,' he replied. 'It wasn't my fault.'

'That may be so, but the fact is we have you on CCTV threatening someone with a knife and we can't ignore that,' DC Burgess told him. 'We need to get the other boys' versions of events too. They might be telling a different story so we need to get to the truth.'

'But I am telling you the truth,' whimpered Keegan.

He started to cry again.

'Am I going to go to prison? What's going to happen to me?'

'I'm afraid I don't know at this stage,' nodded DC Fiddis.

Keegan was hysterical now and I knew that I had to step in.

'Please could you turn the tape off?' I asked them. 'He needs a break.' I was also starting to think I should call Helen and try and get Social Services to organise a solicitor for Keegan.

The officers nodded.

While they were talking among themselves, I turned to Keegan.

'I'm so sorry you had to carry all of that worry around with you,' I told him. 'You must have been really scared.'

He nodded.

For someone who hadn't opened up much at all over the past few weeks, he'd said a lot today. My gut instinct told me that he was telling the truth and it wasn't just him passing the blame on to someone else. I could see that it was genuine fear and remorse in his eyes.

'It's going to be OK,' I reassured him. 'Whatever happens, Helen and I are here to support you. Any judge or court will understand how vulnerable you are and what a hard time you've been going through.'

'Judge?' he gasped, his eyes wide with fear. 'I have to go to a court like on the telly?'

I couldn't lie to him.

'I don't honestly know,' I told him. 'But let's not worry about that now.'

He started to cry again and I put my arms around him. I thought he might push me away but he buried his head into my shoulder and sobbed his heart out.

It took a good ten minutes for him to calm down, his tears slowly subsiding and his breathing returning to normal.

I knew I urgently needed to let Helen know what was happening.

'I need to pop out briefly and make a quick phone call,' I told him. 'Will you be OK?'

He nodded.

The two officers said they'd sit with Keegan.

I went out and rang Helen.

'I really think you need to come down here as soon as possible,' I told her. 'Keegan's admitted everything and I think they're going to charge him.'

'What?' she said, sounding shocked. 'Oh no, I really hoped you were wrong in your suspicions, Maggie.'

'Me too,' I said. 'He's in a real state. It sounds like he's been manipulated by some older boys.'

'I'll be there as soon as I can,' she told me.

When I went back into the interview room, DC Fiddis had got Keegan a sandwich and he was tucking in hungrily.

Helen arrived fifteen minutes later and I went to meet her in reception.

'How is he?' she asked.

'Tired, upset and very frightened,' I told her.

I explained how I'd found the knife in his jacket pocket and then he'd admitted everything – that the older boys had pushed him into robbing the shop.

'I can't believe he had a knife on him, Maggie,' she told me. 'He's twelve!'

'Me neither,' I said. 'I can't believe he's been going through all of this alone and none of us realised until now.'

All I could think about was how scared Keegan must have been.

'Given what's happened, we also need to reassess the situation,' Helen told me.

'What do you mean?' I asked.

'Even if he was coerced into it, Keegan has admitted taking part in a violent crime,' she replied. 'And we know now that he's been walking around with a knife.'

I nodded.

'So we need to think seriously about whether you can have him back in your house,' she continued. 'Is he a risk to Billy and to Cooper? Is he a risk to you?'

'I truly don't feel like he is,' I told her. 'If I was worried then I would say something.'

All I saw was a scared little boy who had made a mistake and been manipulated by some older boys at the most vulnerable time of his life. I had fostered children in the past where I'd realised that they were a genuine danger. There were even a couple of children that I'd asked to be removed the same day they'd arrived with me because of the level of violence they'd shown, and I genuinely felt they were a risk to me and others. One child had punched me in the stomach and another had broken my wrist. On those occasions, the children had overstepped a boundary and I refused to live in fear in my own home, a place where I had a right to be safe. I didn't feel as if any of us were at risk from Keegan. If I had, I'd have spoken up about it.

'I'm happy to continue the placement and keep him with his brothers,' I told her. 'He needs my help and support more than ever to get him through this. He needs stability, not more change.'

I could see Helen wasn't convinced.

'Ordinarily, in a situation like this, you know we wouldn't allow the child to continue in the placement,' Helen told me.

'Helen, I'm begging you, please allow him to come back and live with me,' I said. 'I know he had a knife on him but I truly believe that it was the older boys' influence. They'd threatened him and he didn't know what to do.'

'Do you believe him?' she asked me.

'I really do,' I nodded. 'I can see he's genuinely terrified.'

Keegan's actions against the shopkeeper were so out of character and went against everything his teachers had told us about him.

'I don't think I can make this decision myself,' Helen told me. 'I need to have a chat to my manager about it.'

While she called her manager, I gave Becky a ring to update her. She was as shocked as we all had been.

'Helen's talking about not letting him come back home with me,' I told her, panicked. 'She thinks it might be too much of a risk.'

'What do you think?' she asked me.

'You know me, Becky,' I replied. 'If I thought he was a risk to me or Cooper or Billy, I would tell you.

'The last thing Keegan needs right now is to be moved to a children's home away from his brothers.'

However, I knew ultimately that decision was out of my hands and it was down to Social Services as they had parental responsibility.

When we were both off the phone, Helen and I had another chat.

'I've explained the situation to my manager,' she told me.

She said she wanted to think about it and look at a few options.

'Is she thinking about sending him to a children's home?' I asked, my stomach sinking.

'Quite possibly,' she replied. 'Look, I know it's hard, but I think it's best you head home, Maggie. I'll stay here with Keegan for now and I'll let you know what's happening.'

'What, just leave him?' I gasped.

'I don't know how long it's going to be before my manager gets back to me and the police might want to ask him some more questions,' she told me. 'I know you've got Billy and Cooper to think about too.'

That was true.

'Honestly, I can take it from here,' she told me. 'I'll keep in touch.'

I knew I didn't really have much choice.

'OK, but I feel like I'm abandoning him,' I sighed.

'I'll be with him,' Helen reassured me.

I still felt terrible about it.

Now I had to go back into the interview room and tell Keegan I was leaving.

'Keegan, it's getting late and I need to go back home and check on Billy and Cooper,' I told him gently.

'But why can't I come with you?' he asked, his eyes wide with fear.

'The police have got a few more things they want to check with you,' I replied. 'Helen's going to stay with you.'

I felt so guilty seeing the panic in his eyes.

'You are coming back, aren't you?' he asked. 'You'll come back later and get me?'

I knew I couldn't reassure him because I didn't know the answer. There was a significant risk that Social Services would decide he couldn't come back and live at my house.

'It's going to be fine,' I said, forcing a smile on my face. 'Helen will keep me updated. I'll see you later.'

I managed to hold it together until the door of the interview room closed behind me. Then I burst into tears.

Helen must have seen through my bravado and she followed me out into the corridor.

'Oh Maggie,' she said. 'I could see you were upset.'

'I just feel so awful leaving him,' I told her.

'I will be with him,' she reassured me again. 'I'll call my manager again shortly and I'll keep you posted.'

I knew Social Services ultimately had the final decision about what happened to Keegan and I would have to accept that. But it was so hard leaving the police station not knowing what was going to happen and if I was going to be allowed to keep fostering him.

Tears streamed down my face as I walked towards the taxi that I'd ordered to take me back home.

Was I ever going to see Keegan again? And what on earth was I going to tell his brothers?

SIXTEEN

Fallout

It was after nine by the time the taxi pulled up outside my house. I opened the door as quietly as I could as I didn't want to wake any of the children.

Vicky looked up expectantly as I walked into the kitchen.

'Oh Maggie, you've been ages,' she told me. 'Are you OK?'

'Just about,' I replied, giving her a weak smile. 'Has everyone been OK?' I asked.

'The little ones were shattered so they went down a while ago,' Vicky nodded. 'I hope you don't mind but I put Paige in your bed.'

'No, of course not,' I said. 'I was happy for you to do that.'

I flopped down on one of the kitchen chairs.

'Let me make you a cup of tea and you can tell me what happened,' Vicky told me.

'Thank you,' I said gratefully, suddenly realising how exhausted I felt.

'Do you want something to eat?' she asked. 'I can make you a sandwich if you want?'

'No thanks,' I replied. 'I feel a bit sick, to be honest.'

Vicky made us both a cup of tea and sat back down at the table. I appreciated her not bombarding me with questions as soon as I'd walked in the door.

After a good few minutes, she gently asked how it had gone.

'Where's Keegan?' she asked.

I explained what had happened. How he'd got in with the wrong crowd and was forced to take part in the shop robbery. How I'd found the knife in his jacket pocket while at the station and had handed it to the police.

'Oh, the poor lad,' she sighed. 'He must have been so scared.'

'But as the police pointed out, that's just Keegan's version of events,' I said. 'He might be lying to cover his own back.'

'What do you think?' asked Vicky.

'I believe him. I don't feel as if he's the kind of kid who would want to carry a knife. I think he was manipulated by these older kids.'

Even so, I explained that Social Services were concerned about him coming back to my house.

'Because he had a knife on him, they're worried it's too great a risk,' I said. 'I can understand their fears but I really don't feel like he is.'

'They were talking about sending him to a children's home, Vicky.'

I could feel my eyes filling up with tears again.

'Oh Maggie,' said Vicky, giving me a hug. 'I can see how hard it must have been for you to leave him there at the police station.'

'He looked so small and scared,' I sniffed. 'A children's home isn't what he needs right now. He needs calm, stability and to be with his brothers.'

My Brother's Secret

Vicky passed me a tissue and I dabbed my eyes.

'Do you want me to stay with you tonight?' she asked.

'No, you get home,' I told her. 'You've got Paige to think about. I'll be fine. Helen's with Keegan at the police station and she's going to keep in touch and let me know what's happening.'

'Well, you know where I am if you need me,' she nodded.

'Thank you,' I smiled, patting her hand.

Vicky and I had been there for each other over the years, through all of life's ups and downs, and I really appreciated her support.

She also warned me that Cooper had been asking where Keegan was.

'He's been asking lots of questions but I didn't say anything,' she told me.

'I don't honestly know what I'm going to tell him,' I said.

Due to confidentiality, I couldn't tell Cooper what was happening with his brother. Keegan could tell him himself if he wanted to but it was a breach of his confidentiality if I did. A child's confidentiality was paramount in fostering, even between siblings.

Vicky went upstairs to get Paige while I went to unlock her car for her. A few minutes later, she carried a sleeping Paige, wrapped in a blanket, down the stairs.

She hardly stirred as Vicky lifted her into the back seat and I pulled the seatbelt across her.

'Try and get some sleep and I'll give you a call tomorrow,' Vicky told me.

I knew I wouldn't be able to sleep a wink until I knew where Keegan was going tonight.

As I gently shut the front door, Cooper came down the stairs.

'Where've you been?' he asked. 'Where's Keegan?'

'He's with Helen at the minute,' I told him.

'But when's he coming back?' he questioned.

'I'm not sure, lovey,' I told him. 'They're just sorting a few things out.'

Cooper looked utterly confused but the truth was, I didn't really know what was happening myself. It was a waiting game.

By 10 p.m. I still hadn't heard anything more from Helen. Thankfully, I managed to persuade Cooper to go to bed.

It was half past ten before my phone started ringing. I leapt on it.

'Is everything OK, Helen?' I asked.

'I'm just letting you know that I'm leaving the police station now,' she told me. 'And I'm bringing Keegan back to your house.'

'Really?' I gasped. 'Oh, that's great news.'

It was such a relief.

'My manager wasn't able to secure a place for him anywhere else,' she said. 'So she's agreed that it's OK for him to stay in the placement.'

She'd also called my agency to let them know.

'They're happy for him to come back and stay as long as you are.'

'Absolutely,' I told her. 'Thank you.'

Half an hour later, they were at my front door. Keegan looked pale, tired and terrified but I was so relieved to see him.

I ushered him and Helen into the kitchen.

'Do you need a drink or anything to eat, flower?' I asked him.

He shook his head.

'Do you want to go and get yourself ready for bed then as it's late,' I added. 'I'll come up and see you in a bit.'

'OK,' he replied.

That gave me and Helen a chance to chat.

'What happened with the police?' I asked her.

She explained they wanted to question the other boys and talk to the Crown Prosecution Service.

'They haven't charged him with anything yet but they think they're likely to,' she added. 'They might want to question him again over the next few days but they're going to keep in touch.'

It all felt such a mess.

'Where do we go from here?' I asked her.

We had a chat about safeguarding in the house. I already had all the knives locked away but she advised me to do another sweep of the house and lock away anything sharp such as scissors.

'Do you think there's a risk Keegan might try and sneak out tonight and warn these other boys about the police?' Helen asked me.

'I honestly don't think so,' I told her. 'He seems scared of them and I think the last thing he would want to do is tell them that he'd given their names to the police.'

'Just be vigilant and keep an eye on things,' she told me.

'What about school?' I asked. 'I don't think Keegan would feel safe going back.'

These boys didn't go to his school but they lived near it and hung round the local area.

'Keep him off tomorrow and I'll make an appointment for you and I to go and meet with the school,' she told me.

'OK thanks,' I said.

I saw Helen glance at her watch and I suddenly realised how tired she looked too.

'I'm going to head home now but let's talk tomorrow,' she told me.

'OK,' I nodded. 'Thank you for bringing Keegan back.'

I still felt an overwhelming sense of relief that I'd been allowed to continue the placement and he wasn't on his way to a children's home somewhere.

Once I'd seen Helen out, I went upstairs to check on Keegan.

He was in the bathroom but it was obvious he and Cooper had been talking.

'I told you them knives weren't mine,' Cooper told me as soon as I walked into their bedroom.

'I'm so sorry for accusing you,' I replied. 'I made a big mistake.'

'That's OK,' he nodded. He was remarkably quick to forgive me, but I think he was just relieved his brother was back with him.

I was curious about what he knew.

'Did you know what your brother had got involved in?' I asked him.

He shook his head.

'If I had, I'd have sorted it,' he replied. 'I know who he's talking about and they're not nice lads.'

He paused.

'Is he going to go to prison?' he asked me.

'No, they don't send twelve-year-olds to prison,' I replied. 'But we think it's likely the police are going to charge him and he might have to go to the youth courts.'

Cooper looked upset.

My Brother's Secret

'I should have known,' he sighed. 'I could have stopped it.'

I didn't want Cooper to blame himself.

'None of us realised,' I said. 'Keegan kept it all to himself. I wish he'd told us.'

I felt like kicking myself because I hadn't had a clue. I'd been so focused on Cooper, perhaps I'd missed the signs. But there was nothing in his behaviour that had raised the slightest bit of suspicion.

Just then Keegan came out of the bathroom.

He was already in his pyjamas and he got straight into bed.

'Try and get some sleep,' I told him.

'I'm sorry,' he told me. 'I'm sorry about everything. I thought they were my mates and they liked me.'

'I know,' I nodded. 'Whatever happens, we'll get through it.'

The next morning, I woke up to a text from Helen.

The head can do a 9.30 meeting at school this morning.

I didn't want to leave Keegan on his own in the house after everything that had happened yesterday so I called on Vicky again.

I arranged to drop him at her house on the way to taking Billy and Cooper to school.

Keegan looked shattered as I hauled him out of bed but I could see he was relieved not to be going to school.

Helen met me in reception. Mr Smith, the headteacher, was already there waiting along with Mr Broome, Keegan's head of year.

'We were shocked to hear what had happened,' he said. 'It sounds so out of character for Keegan.'

Like Social Services, their main concern was the knife.

'As you know, if Keegan comes onto the school site with a knife he will be immediately excluded,' Mr Smith told us. 'We don't want to take that risk.'

Helen reassured them that I would be searching Keegan's bag and clothes every morning.

'He understands that this has got to happen and you might want to do the same when he arrives at school,' she told them.

I explained that Keegan had given the boys' names to the police and was terrified of retaliation.

'They don't go to this school but they live in the local area,' I explained. 'Keegan's worried they're going to wait for him and hurt him or try and get revenge somehow.'

'We were hoping we could work with you to put some kind of safeguarding plan in place so Keegan can stay at this school as I think he needs that continuity right now,' Helen continued.

I suggested that I walked both boys to the school entrance every morning to drop them off, then pick them up after school too.

'Is Cooper going to go along with that too?' asked Mr Smith.

'I think he realises the danger to his brother so he'll have to,' nodded Helen.

Rather than Cooper having his bag and his coat searched every morning for knives, it was now going to be Keegan.

They also agreed Keegan could stay in the library at break times and lunchtimes to keep him out of the playground.

'We can't risk any of these boys trying to access the school grounds looking for him,' added Helen.

Later that morning, when I discussed it with Keegan, he seemed shocked that we were sending him back to school.

My Brother's Secret

'But what if they come and find me and try to stab me?' he sighed. 'They'll know I grassed them up to the police.'

'That's not going to happen,' I told him. 'Helen and I have come up with a plan with your teachers to make sure that you're safe. The school's going to tell the office staff and all the other teachers what's happening so if you're ever scared, you can go to any member of staff and get help. They know to look out for anyone suspicious who shouldn't be on the premises.'

However, the next morning I could see Keegan was terrified as I dropped him off. As we walked from the car to the school reception, he was constantly looking around nervously.

'Keegan, it's going to be OK,' I reassured him.

He didn't look very convinced.

'Don't worry, Keegan, if I see any of them lads, I'll get them for you,' nodded Cooper.

'Cooper, I don't think that's the solution,' I told him. 'You need to leave it to the teachers to handle.'

Mr Broome was waiting for Keegan in reception.

'You'll be fine,' I smiled.

I really hoped that he would be. As Billy skipped along next to me, thankfully oblivious to everything that was going on, my mind was firmly on Keegan.

He'll be OK, I told myself. He'll be safe in school.

I also wondered whether we'd hear any more from the police today.

'Look!' yelled Billy suddenly, his eyes wide in wonder.

He'd stopped to look at something on the pavement, which I realised was a slug.

'Oh look, it's all slimy Maggie,' he said, poking it with a stick. 'Can I take it back to your house and it can be my pet?'

I smiled.

'I think we've got lots of slimy slugs in our garden,' I replied. 'Shall we have a look later when we get home?'

He nodded then carried on skipping, his stick still firmly clasped in his hand. Thank goodness for Billy and his sweet observations and childlike innocence. It was just what I needed to take my mind off what was happening with his big brother.

Just after lunchtime my phone rang. My heart raced with panic as I saw the number of Cooper and Keegan's school flash up.

I felt sick when I heard Mr Broome's voice on the other end of the line.

'What's happened?' I garbled. 'Is Keegan OK?'

'We've had a bit of a safeguarding issue,' he replied.

My heart sank. My worst fear had come true.

'Oh no,' I sighed. 'Was it the boys who he told the police about? Please tell me they didn't hurt him?'

Mr Broome went very quiet.

'We did have someone on the school site looking for Keegan,' he replied. 'But it wasn't the boys.

'It was his dad.'

SEVENTEEN

Reunions

'Their dad?' I questioned, totally thrown by this curveball.

It certainly hadn't been what I was expecting.

'Yes, their father Jason turned up at reception demanding to see Cooper and Keegan and take them out of school,' Mr Broome, Keegan's head of year, told me. 'Thankfully our receptionist knew that the boys are in care and she couldn't allow that.'

'Have you contacted their social worker Helen as well?' I asked.

'We're getting hold of her now,' said Mr Broome. 'I just wanted to let you know too as you're both named contacts.'

'What about the boys?' I asked. 'Are they OK? Did they see their dad?'

'They're fine,' he said. 'They were in lessons when he turned up.'

He explained that they'd both been removed from their classrooms and taken to the library as it was in the middle of the school building.

'We thought that was best, just to make sure their dad didn't see them through a classroom window and try to approach them,' he added.

'Did you tell the boys what was going on?' I questioned.

'No,' replied Mr Broome. 'We didn't want to upset or worry them.'

I thought the school had done the right thing, however, I knew Keegan's mind would have gone into overdrive thinking the gang from the estate had turned up looking for him.

'And what about their dad?' I asked. 'Where is he now?'

He explained they'd asked Jason to wait in reception.

'Do you think we need to call the police?' Mr Broome asked.

'If he isn't being aggressive, then I don't think so,' I said.

After all, Jason hadn't been deemed as a risk to the boys.

Part of me was relieved that it hadn't been a gang turning up to try and confront Keegan but equally, I was confused. What was their dad doing back? Why had he turned up now and what did he want?

'I'll ring their social worker and then I'll come up to collect the boys,' I told him.

It was after 2 p.m., so by the time I got there, it would be the end of the school day anyway.

I was about to dial Helen's number when she called me.

'I've just heard what happened at school,' she said. 'That's a turn-up for the books, isn't it? I certainly didn't expect that.'

'I know,' I replied. 'My heart was in my mouth when Mr Broome rang. I thought a group of lads had got into the school and something had happened to Keegan, so it was almost a relief to find out that it was their dad.

'I've arranged to go and pick up the boys,' I added. 'But what happens from here?'

Helen explained that she had been in a meeting when the school had called, so a duty worker had gone up to the school to speak to Jason and see what was going on. She'd checked with Billy's primary school and thankfully he hadn't been there.

'Hopefully they'll persuade Dad to leave the school premises and get him to come into the office to talk to us,' she told me. 'He can't just abandon his kids for months without a word and then turn up out of the blue and expect to see them.'

'What about the boys?' I asked. 'I'm going to drive over to school shortly and pick them up.'

'Maggie, let me contact the school first and make sure that Jason has left before you go and get them,' she added. 'Then when you're back, I'll come round to talk to them and explain what's happened.'

Fifteen minutes after I'd got off the phone to her, she sent me a message.

Dad's left the school premises so the coast is clear. He has my phone number and he's supposed to be calling me to make an appointment.

I collected Billy first as he finished earlier then we drove to Cooper and Keegan's school. I parked up and, as was our new routine, we went to collect them from reception.

I could see them waiting for us.

'Something weird happened today,' Cooper told me as we left the school building. 'I got pulled out of maths and had to wait in the library with Keegan. Miss wouldn't tell me nothing. Do you know what was going off, Maggie?'

'I'm not sure,' I told him.

I knew it wasn't my place to tell them about their dad. That was the kind of information that had to come from their social worker and Helen would talk to them back at my house.

Keegan hadn't said a word up until now but he looked absolutely terrified.

'Do you think it was them lads?' he asked me quietly as we walked to the car. 'I think they came to get me.'

'I don't think so,' I told him. 'Helen's coming round and we can all have a chat with her about it when we get home.'

On the drive back, Billy chatted away to me but the boys were silent.

The boys were at the kitchen table having a drink and a biscuit when Helen arrived. I made us both a cup of tea.

When I sat back down, Billy perched on my lap and started dipping his biscuit into his juice.

'Something happened today that I need to talk to you boys about,' she told them.

Keegan looked like he was about to burst into tears.

'Your dad turned up at school today asking to see you both,' she told them.

'Dad?' gasped Cooper. 'When's he coming round to get us? Maggie, have you got some bags that I can put my stuff in?'

'Cooper, I'm afraid it's not as simple as that,' Helen told him. 'I haven't had a chance yet to have a proper chat to him but he'll be coming to my office to have a meeting with me.'

Keegan hadn't said anything so far and I could tell that he was slowly taking it all in.

'Do you think he knows what's happened with the police?' he asked me anxiously.

My Brother's Secret

'I don't think so,' I replied. 'He hasn't been in touch with anyone at Social Services before now.'

Billy just looked confused.

'Is my daddy coming to live at this house?' he asked me.

'No, he's not going to come and live here, sweetie,' I replied.

'Billy, don't be stupid, we're going to go and live with Dad,' Cooper told him. 'We'll just go back to our old flat.'

'Cooper, that's not something that's going to happen at the moment,' Helen warned him. 'We're going to chat to your dad then hopefully we can arrange for you all to see him in a few days.'

'But that ain't fair,' he replied. 'He's our dad, we can go and live with him if we want.'

'It's not as simple as that,' I told him. 'Helen needs to check that it's something your dad also wants. And if he does, they need to make sure that your dad can look after you and that he's not going to leave again in another few weeks.'

Cooper looked cross, Billy seemed confused and Keegan was just very quiet.

After that, Billy went to watch TV in the front room and Keegan and Cooper retreated to their bedrooms.

'I'm not sure how that news went down,' I shrugged.

'At least they know,' Helen replied. 'I'll speak to Jason and hopefully then we'll have more of an idea of what he's thinking.'

We also talked about the police. We were still waiting for them to get in touch to let us know if Keegan was going to be charged.

'Have you heard anything from DC Fiddis?' Helen asked me.

'Not a peep,' I shrugged.

I knew it was preying on Keegan's mind and it was certainly preying on mine. I could tell Keegan was worried about telling his dad what he'd got involved in.

'It's all very unknown right now,' said Helen as she left. 'But hopefully things will start to become a bit clearer in the next few days. Keep in touch, Maggie.'

After she'd gone, I sat with Billy in the front room for a while. I wondered what he made of it all. He must have been so confused but he didn't ask me any more questions.

Cooper and Keegan didn't say anything else either. It was only after dinner, when I was tidying up the dishes and the other boys were elsewhere in the house, that I noticed Keegan was hanging around the kitchen.

'Can I get you anything, flower?' I asked him. 'Do you want a yoghurt for pudding or an apple maybe?'

'No, I'm OK,' he mumbled.

Then he paused and I could tell there was something he wanted to ask me.

'What is it, sweetie?' I asked. 'You look upset.'

He stared at the floor.

'I don't want to go back and live with my dad,' he said quietly.

'Why not?' I questioned.

'I can't go back to our flat ever again,' he said, his eyes filling with tears. 'If I go back to our estate, them boys will kill me. They know I grassed them up and they'll stab me. I can't ever go back there – please don't let them make me.'

He started to cry and I could tell that he was genuinely frightened. I led him to the sofa and sat down with him.

My Brother's Secret

'Please don't worry,' I told him, rubbing his back. 'Helen understands the situation and we would never ever do anything that would put you in any danger.'

'But does that mean we'd never be allowed to live with Dad?' he asked.

'Not necessarily,' I said. 'If your dad's saying he wants you back and he shows Helen that he's really committed and Social Servies agree, then they might be able to help him find a new flat somewhere else.'

I knew the only issue with that was it often took a while to find a new property.

'It's not going to be straight away though,' I told him. 'Your dad's got to talk to Helen about quite a lot of things before they can decide whether that's going to be allowed to happen.'

Keegan seemed a little bit calmer but I knew he was very anxious about the police and these other boys. So much was unknown at the minute and I just wish I knew what was going to happen.

Thankfully the next day, everyone seemed OK.

'Is Daddy coming to my school today?' Billy asked as I walked him to his classroom.

'No, lovey,' I said. 'Hopefully Helen will arrange for you to see your daddy soon but she will tell you when.'

We didn't even know at this stage whether Jason was prepared to engage with Social Services, so I was surprised when Helen called me that afternoon.

'Jason came into the office to see me earlier,' she said.

He hadn't exactly got a track record for reliability so I was surprised but pleased that he'd turned up.

'It turns out that he's split up with the girlfriend and he's back here now,' she said.

'Where's he living?' I asked.

'He's back in his old flat,' she told me. 'He didn't tell housing he was leaving so it's still been paid for these past few weeks.'

He hadn't registered for any benefits where his girlfriend lived and had been doing cash-in-hand jobs so it hadn't flagged on the system that he'd moved.

'So what's he thinking?' I asked.

'He says that he wants his boys back,' Helen told me. 'In his mind, he didn't abandon them. He says he told Social Services that he was leaving so he knew they'd be OK. He said that he'd missed them and he was hoping to persuade his girlfriend to change her mind and let them come and live with him eventually before they'd split.'

His interpretation of events had been totally different to ours.

'I did point out that we'd tried multiple times to get in touch with him, and that the boys hadn't had any kind of contact with him since he left but he didn't think there was anything wrong with that,' she added.

However, whatever had happened in the past, he was their dad and he had a right to see the boys and have a chance to prove himself to them and Social Services.

'I've set up a contact session for two days' time,' Helen told me. 'That's the earliest I could get a slot at a centre.'

If Helen was there supervising the session, it meant she could see the interactions between Jason and the boys and get more of an idea of him as a parent and his relationship with them.

'I've explained to Jason that this isn't something that's going to happen quickly, if at all,' Helen added. 'He was under the misapprehension that he could just walk back into their lives and pick up where he left off but I told him it wasn't as easy as that.'

Social Services would need reassurance that he could cope with looking after the boys and, also, that he wasn't going to up and leave again.

'Did you tell him about the trouble Keegan was in?' I asked her.

'I had to,' she replied. 'He needed to know. He was shocked and I think for the first time, he realised what the impact of him leaving might have had on the children.'

That afternoon, I told Cooper and Keegan that the plan was to see their dad in a couple of days.

'I'm not saying anything to Billy at the moment just in case a problem arises and your dad isn't able to come,' I told them. 'So please don't talk about it in front of him.'

Cooper seemed pleased.

'If my dad says he's going to turn up, then he will,' he nodded.

I hope so, I thought to myself. I didn't want the boys to feel as if they'd been abandoned all over again.

On the day of the contact session, by the time I'd collected all three boys from school, I'd received a text from Helen saying Jason had arrived at the contact centre. It meant I could finally break the news to Billy.

'Guess what?' I told him. 'We're going to go and see your daddy.'

'Now?' asked Billy.

'Yep,' I nodded. 'We're going to go to a special place called a contact centre to see him.'

It was at a centre that I'd been to several times over the years – a slightly run-down eighties brick building in the middle of a housing estate. It was all harsh strip lighting, peeling paintwork and toys that had seen better days. But it was small, not too intimidating and it gave children a safe space to see their birth parents.

After we'd been buzzed in by a contact worker, I saw Helen with a man who I assumed was Jason waiting in one of the rooms with the door open.

He was tall and skinny with baggy jeans with holes in them and a scruffy jacket. His neck was covered in tattoos and I could see he had a cigarette tucked behind his ear.

I hung back in reception but Cooper went in to see him.

'Dad!' he said.

'Hiya, mate,' said Jason, slapping him on the back as if he had run into an old friend at the pub.

Billy ran straight in to see him too.

'My daddy,' he said, wrapping his arms around his legs. 'Daddy, Daddy.'

'Alright, Bills, how are you doing?' said Jason, patting him on the head.

While his two brothers had gone straight to Jason, Keegan had hung back near the door.

'Hello, mate,' said Jason, walking towards him.

'Hi, Dad,' said Keegan quietly.

He knew that his dad would have been told about what had happened with the police and I could tell he was worried about how he was going to react.

'The lady from the Social told me what's been going on,' he said. 'You're in a bit of trouble, aren't you, mate? I never thought you'd be up to anything like that.'

Keegan nodded.

'Don't worry, son. I'll sort it,' he told him. 'I know you're not a bad lad.'

I'd been watching all of this unfold from the reception area. I didn't know how Jason would react to seeing me and I didn't want to cause any issues in front of the boys. They only had an hour and I didn't want to disturb their contact time.

Just then, Billy came running out.

'Maggie, my dad's in there,' he told me. 'Come and see him.'

'I'll come in before we go and say hi to your daddy then,' I told him.

I sat in reception and did some paperwork to help distract me from wondering how things were going in the contact room.

Five minutes before the session was due to end, Helen popped her head out.

'Do you want to come in for a minute?' she asked.

Billy was on the floor playing with some Hot Wheels cars and tracks and Keegan was with him. Cooper was sat on the sofa with Jason.

'This is Maggie,' Helen told him. 'She's the one who's been looking after the boys.'

Jason nodded but didn't get up.

'You've got three lovely lads there,' I smiled.

'Yeah, they're alright ain't they?' he said. 'I just want 'em back with me now.'

Helen was quick to step in.

'We've just been talking about that,' she said. 'And I was explaining to Jason and the boys that it's not something that can happen overnight. There are a lot of things we need to discuss first.'

*

After I took the boys home, Helen gave me a call.

'How did the session go?' I asked her.

'I think it went well,' she said. 'I know it wouldn't be yours or my way of parenting but I think Jason genuinely cares about the boys in his own way.'

At contact sessions, it was important to look at the children's reactions to their dad. He might not have been into big displays of affection but the boys clearly had a connection with him. They weren't scared of him, he wasn't nasty to them and I could tell that he did care for them.

'I'm just worried both Jason and the boys think it's a done deal that they're going to be going back to live with him,' she told me. 'That's certainly not the case.'

Before he left, there had been concern that he wasn't coping and then he'd walked out on them. It wasn't a given that Jason would be allowed to have the boys back. But would Social Services give him a second chance?

Even if they did, he had a lot to prove first.

EIGHTEEN

Rough Justice

It was lovely to answer the phone and hear Louisa's voice at the other end.

'I'm so sorry, lovey,' I told her. 'I've been so tied up with the boys I feel like I haven't caught up properly with you or Edie for ages.'

'Don't worry, Maggie, I know what it's like,' she replied.

Although I hadn't told her the ins and outs of what had happened with Keegan, she was perceptive enough to know a lot had been going on over the past few weeks.

'Let's try and meet up on your day off this week,' I suggested.

Thankfully she was feeling much better and her scan was only a couple of weeks away now.

'The boys' birth dad is back on the scene so I'm taking them to contact a couple of times a week after school. But apart from that, I'm free.'

'Oh wow,' she said. 'How's it going?'

'OK so far,' I told her.

Jason had made it clear to Social Services that he wanted to have his boys back. He was still of the view that he hadn't abandoned them because he'd told Social Services that he was going. Even so, Helen had explained that he would need to have a six-week parenting assessment to reassure them that he could do it.

There was also Keegan's involvement with the police to think about. So much else had been happening, I'd almost put it to the back of my mind.

Until a few days later when Helen phoned me.

'DC Fiddis just rang,' she said. 'They want us to bring Keegan to the police station after school tomorrow.'

'That can't be a good sign, can it?' I asked. 'If they weren't going to charge him, I'd have thought they'd tell you that on the phone.'

'We'll have to see,' she said. 'It could be that they're not going to charge him but they want to give him a good talking to and a caution.'

Keegan had been really fragile recently. He was still living in fear of the boys from the estate coming to get him and he wasn't sleeping properly.

I didn't tell him about the police until the following morning before school. I didn't want him to worry overnight and have an even more disturbed sleep. I'd already arranged for Vicky to come round straight after school to look after Billy and Cooper.

I managed to grab a quiet moment with him in the hallway while the other boys were getting into the car.

'The police have asked me and Helen to take you to the police station after school today,' I told him.

'Why?' he asked, alarmed.

'I don't know, flower,' I replied. 'I can only assume that they've made a decision about whether to charge you or not.'

He looked absolutely terrified.

'Try not to worry,' I told him. 'We don't know what they're going to say yet and Helen and I will be with you.'

However, that afternoon Mr Broome called me.

'We've had to take Keegan out of class as he's been really tearful,' he told me.

'There's a lot going on at the moment,' I explained.

When I picked him up later, he looked drained.

He insisted on staying in the car when I dropped Cooper and Billy at home and let Vicky and Paige in. He hardly said a word on the drive to the police station.

'Keegan, whatever happens, you will get through this,' I told him. 'The police know everything you've been through in your personal life and how you've been manipulated by these older boys.'

He nodded but he didn't look convinced.

Helen was waiting for us in reception. As was usual for a police station, it was noisy and packed with all sorts of people from all walks of life. Keegan suddenly looked so young and vulnerable. Helen and I chatted among ourselves but he hardly said a word.

Eventually, DC Fiddis came out to meet us.

'Hi, Keegan,' he said. 'Come on through.'

We followed him for ages down a labyrinth of corridors until he finally showed us into another interview room like the one we'd been in a few weeks ago. Helen and I sat either side of Keegan, and DC Fiddis had a file on the table in front of him.

'Keegan, as you know we've been talking to the Crown Prosecution Service about your case and we've been waiting for them to make a decision . . .'

I could tell Keegan was scared but I could suddenly feel my own heart racing in my chest. I didn't realise how much I had been dreading this meeting too. He'd been through so much and, inside, I was desperately willing them to let him off with a caution.

'The CPS do feel there's enough evidence for us to charge you,' DC Fiddis continued.

My stomach sank.

'But that's not fair,' he blurted out. 'I told you I didn't mean it and them boys made me do it.'

I could hear the desperation and panic in his voice.

'Keegan, listen to what DC Fiddis is saying,' Helen urged him.

'They felt the offences were too serious to let you off with a caution,' he continued. 'So you're going to be charged with one count of robbery and another count of possessing a bladed weapon. Is there anything you want to ask me?'

Keegan looked stunned.

'Are they going to put me in prison?' he muttered.

'Children don't go to prison,' DC Fiddis reassured him. 'You'll have to appear at the youth court in ten days' time and they'll decide what will happen. I'm sure Social Services will sort you out with a solicitor and they will talk you through everything.'

Keegan turned to me.

'You said it was gonna be OK,' he snapped.

'And it will be,' I assured him. 'Helen and I will support you through this. Your solicitor will be able to tell the court everything you've been through.'

My Brother's Secret

While Helen sat with Keegan, I went and had a quick word with the DC.

'What about the other boys that Keegan named?' I asked him. 'Are they facing court too?'

'I'm afraid when we questioned them, they denied any involvement in the incident and we don't have enough evidence to charge them,' he explained. 'Unfortunately we can't confirm their identities as the CCTV footage of the incident isn't clear.'

It was the knife that I'd found in Keegan's jacket that was the proof they needed to link him to the crime.

We then had to take Keegan to a counter so he could be formally charged and read his rights. While a custody sergeant read out the charges to him, tears trickled down his face.

'I'll sort him out a solicitor as soon as I can,' Helen told me.

I think she was as surprised as I was that the police and the CPS had decided to take this further, knowing everything they did about Keegan's involvement.

Over the next few days, I tried to prepare Keegan so he'd know what to expect. I'd been to the youth court several times over the years with various foster children.

The youth court was part of the local magistrate's court complex but was designed to be less intimidating than an adult court. It was a closed court so wasn't open to the public and only people involved in the hearing could be there. Everyone sat on the same level; there was no dock and everyone referred to each other by their first names.

I suggested that he wear his white school shirt and trousers.

'That will look smart,' I told him.

The court didn't sit until 10.30 a.m. so fortunately that meant that I could drop Billy and Cooper at school and still get to the court early enough to go through everything with Keegan's solicitor.

As the week had gone on, Keegan had become quieter and more clingy.

The night before the court case, I made him a hot chocolate and sat with him downstairs.

'Do you want to talk about it?' I asked him.

He shook his head.

'I can see how scared you are but whatever happens tomorrow, it's going to be OK,' I told him. 'Helen and I will be with you and whatever the outcome, we're not going to disappear, we'll still be around.'

'My dad said he's coming too,' Keegan told me.

'That would be nice, but let's see,' I replied. 'Something might come up that means he can't make it.'

I didn't want him to rely on Jason turning up and then fall to pieces even more if he didn't show up.

'If Dad said he'll be here, he will,' he said firmly.

He was also worried about his teachers.

'I don't want them to know I have to go to court,' he told me.

'Only Mr Broome and your headteacher Mr Smith know because you needed the day off,' I replied.

'I don't want anyone at school talking to me about it,' he said.

I could see just how ashamed he was of what had happened.

*

On the morning of the court case, the bags under Keegan's eyes told me that he'd hardly slept and he refused to eat any breakfast.

'I feel sick,' he said.

'Listen, I know you're anxious but at least try and eat a piece of toast.'

But he just picked at the crust before pushing it away.

At the magistrate's court we went through security and then headed to the youth court. Helen was there, along with a woman with short dark hair in a smart grey suit.

'This is Alison,' she told us. 'The solicitor who's going to represent Keegan at the hearing today.'

We hadn't met her before although Helen had been through everything with her and given her information about Keegan's background.

'Hi, Keegan,' she said, giving him a smile and it was a relief to see she had a warm, comforting nature.

Helen took Keegan to get a drink from the vending machine while I had a quick chat to her.

'He's very nervous and anxious,' I told her. 'The poor lad's convinced he's going to go to prison despite us telling him they won't do that to him.'

I was curious about what Keegan's punishment could be.

'What sort of sentence could he get for these charges?' I asked.

'They're serious offences,' she said. 'Especially knife crime, which the courts take a very tough stance on. So they can carry anything from six months detention to four years.'

She must have seen the shock on my face.

'But they are Keegan's first offences and I know from the

notes I've had from Social Services that there are a lot of extenuating circumstances that I'll urge them to consider.'

'I've only known him a few months but I truly believe he is a good lad,' I told her. 'He was manipulated by the wrong crowd who got him at his most vulnerable.'

When Keegan came back, Alison calmly talked him through everything that would happen in the court.

'It will be a district judge presiding over the court today,' she told him. 'That's a lady called Jan.'

She explained how Jan would talk him through the offences that he'd been accused of and ask him if he was going to plead guilty or not guilty. Alison wanted to make sure that Keegan understood what they each meant.

'I did do it,' he nodded. 'But I didn't want to. The other boys made me. They said they'd hurt me if I didn't do what they said.'

'I know,' nodded Alison. 'And I will stress that to the judge. And she will also take into account the fact that you've told the truth and are admitting that you were responsible,' she added.

Suddenly, the door to the youth court opened and a clerk called us in.

'Is it happening now?' Keegan asked, his eyes wide with fear.

'Yes, we have to go in,' I told him. 'Remember, it's going to be OK. We're all here for you.'

The court itself was more like a large room. It had a wooden bench where the judge sat and then there was a long wooden desk facing it with a row of blue chairs behind it.

The clerk guided us to one side of it. Helen and I sat either side of Keegan and Alison sat at the end. He kept turning around in his seat and I realised he was looking out for his dad.

My Brother's Secret

Suddenly a door at the back of the court opened up and a woman who looked to be in her sixties walked out. She was wearing a navy blue suit but not a formal gown.

Jan introduced herself to Keegan. then talked him through who everyone in the court was, from the clerk, to the CPS solicitor who would outline the case for the Crown, to the man from the Youth Justice Service.

She was just about to start when the door behind us suddenly opened and Jason was stood there in a shiny grey suit that looked about three sizes too big for him.

'Sorry I'm late,' he said. 'The buses were a nightmare.'

'Dad,' smiled Keegan.

'I told you I'd come, mate,' he said to him, sitting on the row behind us.

Alison explained to Jan who Helen and I were and introduced Jason.

'Stand up please, Keegan,' asked Jan.

Keegan looked at me for reassurance and I nodded.

First of all, she read out the charges to him.

'Keegan, do you understand what you're being accused of?' Jan asked him.

He nodded.

'But I didn't do it,' he blurted. 'Them boys made me.'

Alison put her hand on his shoulder.

'Keegan, we'll go through all of that shortly but listen to what Jan is saying.'

Then she asked him whether he wanted to plead guilty or not guilty.

'Guilty,' he said quietly, bowing his head in shame. 'I did do it but I didn't mean it.'

'You can sit back down now,' Jan told him.

'Well done,' I whispered, giving his arm a squeeze.

Then it was the turn of the prosecution solicitor to outline the charges.

Keegan quietly sobbed while she described the robbery that had taken place, showed the CCTV footage and explained how the knife had been found in Keegan's pocket at the police station.

Jan nodded and took notes.

Then it was the defence solicitor's turn. Alison stood up.

'Your Lordship, Keegan is a child who has consistently shown good behaviour and got good results in school and has never been involved in anything like this before.

'This incident happened at a time of great turbulence, stress and grief in his life.'

I squeezed Keegan's hand as Alison outlined what he'd been through. How his mum had died nearly three years ago, how he'd struggled to make friends at school and become a bit of a loner. She talked about how his dad had struggled to cope and eventually abandoned them and how they'd been taken into care.

Hearing that, Jason suddenly piped up from the row behind us.

'I didn't abandon them!' he shouted. 'I told the Social that I was going. But I'm back now, so Keegan and my other boys are gonna live with me,' he added.

'Thank you,' said Jan. 'I'll make a note of that.'

We waited anxiously as Jan looked through the notes that she'd made.

'Keegan, please will you stand up for me?' she asked him eventually.

Helen and I looked at each other.

My Brother's Secret

This was it.

I could see Keegan's body trembling next to me and a knot had formed in my stomach.

Jan cleared her throat.

'Keegan, I've read the charges and seen the evidence against you,' she told him. 'You have to understand that these are very grave offences, especially for someone as young as you and we have to take knife crime in particular very seriously.'

She paused.

'But I have also heard everything you've been through in your personal life and I appreciate that's a lot to cope with at such a young age. It's clear to me that these incidents have happened at a time that you were extremely vulnerable and it sounds like the other perpetrators took advantage of that.'

I held my breath.

Please, please be lenient on him.

'So today I'm going to let you off with a discharge.'

Keegan looked at me, confused.

'It means the court has decided that the experience of coming here today is enough of a punishment,' she explained.

I felt my shoulders sag with sheer relief and I could tell by the look on Helen's face that she felt the same.

'I hope you will reflect on your actions of that night, Keegan, and will come to realise that carrying a knife, even under duress, could put yourself and others at risk,' she added.

'I do,' he nodded. 'I promise I won't do it ever again.'

As part of his discharge, he had to do some sessions with the Youth Justice team on knife crime and gangs. After she had told us everything Keegan needed to do, Jan left the court.

'Come on, let's get out of here,' said Helen.

As soon as we walked out of the court, Keegan started to cry.

'You got off, son,' Jason told him. 'Why are you crying?'

But I could see it was through sheer relief. All the stress and the worry of the past few weeks had suddenly disappeared and I could tell it was like a weight had been lifted.

'It's finally over,' I smiled, putting my arm around him. 'Let's go home.'

NINETEEN

Second Chances

Pacing up and down the hospital waiting room, I glanced at the clock on the wall. They seemed to have been in there for ages and worry had started to creep in.

Suddenly, the door to the consulting room opened and Charlie stood there. My heart dropped when I saw that Louisa wasn't with him.

'Is everything OK?' I asked anxiously.

'Come and see for yourself,' he told me, gesturing for me to go in.

I walked in to find Louisa lying on the bed. The female sonographer was running the ultrasound probe over her stomach, which was covered in a slimy gel.

'Have a look, Maggie,' smiled Louisa, pointing to the monitor.

There, on the screen in black and white, was the tiniest, most perfectly formed baby.

'Meet your new grandchild,' Louisa said.

'Oh wow,' I gasped. 'And everything's fine?'

'Yes, baby looks healthy and has a strong heartbeat,' smiled the sonographer. 'And all the measurements look spot on for thirteen weeks.'

'He or she has been doing somersaults in there the whole time,' grinned Charlie.

It was such a huge relief.

'That's wonderful news,' I told them, tears pricking my eyes. 'I'm so, so happy for you both.'

I gave Louisa a hug.

'Maggie, are you crying?' she teased.

'I'm just excited that I'm going to be a nana again,' I replied. 'And I know Edie's going to make an amazing big sister.'

After all the ups and downs of the past few months, it was nice to have some happy news for once.

While the sonographer printed out some scan pictures for them, Louisa wiped the gel off and did her trousers up.

'These are already getting too tight,' she said.

'You'll have to get out your jeans with the big stretchy panel,' I told her.

'I loved my maternity jeans,' she smiled. 'They were so comfy.'

It was nice to see her happy and smiling again and now she knew everything was OK with the baby, it was like a weight had been lifted. They were going to go home and tell Edie the news and show her the scan pictures. She was going to be so excited.

'Thank you for letting me come in and have a little peak,' I said.

'I thought you could do with a bit of cheering up,' she replied. 'I know the last few weeks have been full on with the boys.'

My Brother's Secret

It had been a massive relief to get the court proceedings out of the way and for Keegan to know that he wasn't facing any more punishment. Once a week after school, he did a session with the Youth Justice team. They talked to him about all sorts of things, such as knife crime and peer pressure, but they'd also discuss what was going on in his own life, such as how he was getting on at school and what he felt about his dad being back.

'Did you find it useful?' I'd asked him when I went to pick him up after the first session.

'I know knives are bad,' he'd told me. 'I only had them because those boys threatened to hurt me if I didn't do what they said.'

Keegan said he never wanted to touch another knife again and I honestly believed him. I could see how humiliating he found it to be searched when he arrived at school every morning and he hated that I regularly checked their bedroom for knives, but he knew it was something I had to do. Even though we'd reassured him, the anxiety about seeing the boys from the estate was still there. Whenever we were around school or walking to the car, he was constantly looking over his shoulder.

Meanwhile, Cooper's behaviour had improved a lot. He was concentrating more at school and, in a strange way, I think that it had helped that Keegan was the one in trouble for a change and that he wasn't the 'bad one'. I could see how much it had meant to him when I'd apologised for assuming the knives were his. I think there was also a new element of trying to impress his dad.

Cooper was continuing to have sessions with his support worker, Jordan. He still complained about it but I could tell that he liked Jordan and he did talk to him and share what was going on in his life.

Jason was being encouraged to open up more too. He was now a couple of weeks into his parenting assessment with Social Services and things were going OK. He was having two contact sessions a week with the boys after school as well as doing separate sessions with Helen. They'd discuss what made a good parent and how important it was to give children continuity and stability through things such as clean clothes, good food, being available for them and spending time with them. She'd also talked to him about his own childhood and if he'd had these things in his life. Was he parenting like he'd been parented or could he move forward and learn new ways?

Ever since he'd come back on the scene, Jason had continued to insist that he hadn't abandoned the boys because he'd told Social Services that he was going.

'I think he's finally realising the truth,' Helen told me. 'He's starting to understand and acknowledge the sense of abandonment the boys must have felt when he left.'

I still couldn't predict what was going to happen with Jason but he was trying and that was all that mattered right now.

As we were going into the third week of the assessment, Helen was keen to move things on and give Jason more responsibility.

'Instead of him seeing the boys at the contact centre, I'm going to suggest that he collects them from school and takes them out for tea somewhere,' she told me.

He had to take them out as it wasn't safe to take Keegan back to his flat.

My Brother's Secret

I was slightly nervous about it as it was the first unsupervised contact that Jason had had. Up until now, myself, Helen or a contact worker had always been with him at the contact centre to be at the session and check that the boys were OK.

'Do you trust him?' I asked Helen.

'If he's going to get the boys back, then we have to,' she said.

There was no suggestion that Jason was going to run off with them or hurt them, so we had to let him prove himself.

It was late when he dropped the boys back at my house but it seemed to have gone well.

'Sorry, we had to get two buses to get back here,' Jason told me.

He'd taken them out to a café in town for burger and chips and the boys seemed happy.

The one big obstacle that Jason faced to getting the boys back was housing. If he convinced Social Services to let them come back and live with him, it couldn't be at their old flat because of Keegan. Social Services had been to the housing department with Jason to apply for a new property but the issue was, it could sometimes take six to twelve months for something suitable to come up.

One afternoon when I went to pick the boys up from contact, Billy ran up to me.

'My daddy's got a new house,' he told me excitedly.

I looked at Jason, who was just wandering out of the contact room.

'Yeah, I got a flat,' he nodded. 'It's a private let but they said they'll take benefits. I'm signing for it tomorrow.'

'That's great news,' I smiled.

It was another positive step forward. I chatted about it to the boys in the car on the way home.

'Dad says it's over the other side of town so we'd have to change schools if we lived with him,' Cooper told me.

'How do you feel about that?' I asked him.

'I ain't bothered,' he shrugged.

Billy seemed excited too. It was only Keegan who had remained quiet. Out of the three of them, I thought he would be the one most pleased about potentially moving out of the area and changing schools.

Later that evening, he wandered into the kitchen while I was making an apple crumble for pudding. I was about to rub the butter, sugar and flour together to make the crumble topping.

'Can I do it?' he asked.

'Course you can,' I smiled, pushing the bowl over to him. 'I hate that bit.'

I showed him how to rub the mixture together with his fingertips. While he did that, I washed and dried a few pots and pans. At first, we worked away next to each other in comfortable silence.

'Am I doing it right?' he asked, showing me the bowl.

'That's perfect,' I smiled. 'You're doing a great job.'

He paused and I could tell there was something else he wanted to say.

'Are we definitely gonna go back and live with our dad?' he asked me, staring down at the mixing bowl.

'I wouldn't say it's definite at this stage but it's looking quite likely,' I told him. 'Your dad's still got a lot to prove but he seems very determined to do it.'

There was one question that I needed to know the answer to.

'Do you want to go back and live with your dad, Keegan?' I asked him.

Cooper and Billy had been very vocal about the fact that that was what they wanted but I'd never heard Keegan come out and say it.

'I think so,' he shrugged. 'I'm just scared it will be like the last time.'

'It sounded like your dad was struggling after your mum died?'

He shrugged.

'Things were OK until he found a girlfriend, then he just went off a lot,' he said. 'Me and Cooper had to do the food and the washing and sort everything out but we didn't know how to do it.'

My heart broke for him.

'That must have been tough,' I nodded.

'What happens if he does it again?' he questioned. 'If he leaves, can we come back here?'

It was a hard one for me to answer because in all likelihood I'd have another placement by then. And we wouldn't want to move the boys into their dad's flat if we thought there was a risk of him leaving them again.

'Social Services have given your dad a second chance to prove himself,' I told Keegan. 'But if the same thing did happen again then there would be no more chances. And if they think there's any risk at all of your dad doing that, they'll tell him he can't have you back.'

I also reassured him that even if they did go back and live with Jason, they would have lots of support.

'Social Services are not going to wash their hands of you just because you're back living with your dad,' I told him. 'Helen would call and check in with you and there will always be someone you can talk to if you're worried or concerned. They'll also make sure that your dad has plenty of help if he's struggling.'

I also reassured him that if he moved schools, Social Services would make sure that he had a member of staff that he could go to if he was feeling worried or anxious.

'Does that all sound OK?' I asked him and he nodded.

I hoped in some small way I had reassured him.

I really did hope that Jason would stay true to his word and put his kids' needs first because if he didn't, he would lose them for good. I didn't want to see the boys have to go through that all over again. But it was in his hands now.

As the end of the parenting assessment drew near, it was time for another LAC meeting at Social Services. This time, Jason had been invited to attend.

It was an important meeting as I knew big decisions were going to be made about the boys' future. Their IRO, Harriet, was chairing things again.

'So when can I get my lads back?' Jason asked her. 'I get the keys to my new place next week so I can go and get them then.'

'I'm afraid it's not going to be as straightforward as that,' Harriet warned him. 'We haven't made a formal decision about the boys' future yet.'

'But I'm getting them back, right?' asked Jason.

I was starting to panic. He wasn't doing himself any favours here.

'You're still in the process of completing a parenting assessment,' Harriet told him. 'And we need to talk about how it's going.'

'It's going good,' Jason nodded. 'I'm allowed 'em on my own now aren't I, Helen?'

She nodded.

'The boys have been out with Jason now a few times and things have gone well,' she said.

Then it was my turn to address the meeting.

'What are your thoughts, Maggie?' Harriet asked me.

For the past few days, I'd been going over everything in my mind and thinking about what I might say at this meeting. At first, I'd had my doubts about Jason but slowly I'd felt more reassured, especially after my chat with Keegan. He was trying to make amends for the choices he'd made in the past.

'The boys have got a positive relationship with their dad,' I told her. 'I think he's managed to win back their trust and whenever he's supposed to have turned up, he has.'

I talked about how he'd come to court to support Keegan and how he seemed determined to get them back.

Jason gave me a thumbs up across the table.

Then Helen talked about her thoughts.

'If Jason does have the boys back to live with him, there will be ongoing support,' she told Harriet. 'He'll still continue to have sessions with Social Services and we'll also check in with the children regularly about how things are going.'

But I could see Jason shaking his head out of the corner of my eye.

'If I get my lads back, I don't need the Social sticking their noses in my business no more,' he shrugged. 'I'm not having that. My boys want to be with me now and I'm their dad.'

'Jason, we don't want things to go back to how they were last time,' Helen told him. 'We need to make sure that you're all coping and if you're not, we can help.'

'If this is going to work, you're going to have to agree to ongoing input from Social Services,' Harriet added.

I wanted to lean over to Jason and urge him not to be so stubborn.

'You didn't see the three broken little boys who arrived at my house all those months ago,' I told him. 'They felt alone and sad and they had no idea where their dad had gone and none of us could tell them.

'And they've really struggled,' I continued. 'Cooper's had serious behavioural issues and was almost excluded from school. And, as you know, Keegan was in real danger. And a lot of that happened because they were lost and vulnerable and felt abandoned.'

I'd probably spoken out of turn but I felt it needed to be said.

Jason looked stunned. He put his head in his hands.

'I'm sorry,' he sighed. 'I was thinking about myself and not my boys. I want them to be happy.'

'That's what we want too,' Helen told him. 'So please agree to work with us, not against us.'

'OK,' he nodded. 'I'll do it.'

Then it was time for us to make a decision.

'Jason, if you're prepared to continue to show your ongoing commitment to the boys and work with Social Services, then I think we're all in agreement that they can go back and live with you,' Harriet told him.

Helen and I nodded.

'Thank you,' he said. 'I promise you and my lads that I won't let them down.'

My Brother's Secret

I really hoped that it would work out – both for the boys' sake and for Jason's. I'm sure it hadn't been easy being left to bring up three boys on his own, but with that ongoing help and support, hopefully he would cope this time.

Helen came round after school to break the news to the boys.

'We had a meeting today,' she told them. 'And we decided that you can all go back and live with your dad.'

'Yes!' said Cooper, punching the air.

'We're going to Daddy's new house?' asked Billy, obviously trying to get things straight in his mind.

'That's right,' I said. 'It's your new house now too.'

I glanced over at Keegan and he gave me a brave smile.

'Happy?' I asked him and he nodded.

As was usual when children moved back to their birth parents, things suddenly picked up the pace. Jason got the keys to his new flat and a mate with a van helped him to move all his furniture from the old place.

'It's not in bad nick,' Jason told me. 'It don't need no painting or nothin'.'

Just like at my house, Cooper and Keegan would share a bedroom and Billy would have his own room.

The boys did one overnight stay before the full move and I spent most of it worrying about how it was going. When they came back the next day, they seemed happy.

'I slept in my old bed!' Billy told me. 'And we had the same settee.'

Even Keegan seemed happy. I think seeing the flat had helped him realise that this was a new start. He would be far away from his old flat and school and the gang that had preyed on his vulnerabilities. He didn't have to look over his shoulder any more.

Over the next few days, I helped the boys pack their things ready to take over to their new home. They'd accumulated quite a few clothes over the past few months and I packed a separate case full of towels and bedding that I thought might come in handy for Jason.

Their last day with me was a Saturday and that afternoon, I was going to drive them over to their new flat and had bought some pizzas for tea.

We packed up the car with the last of their things.

'Right,' I told them. 'Let's go.'

The boys were excited to show me their new flat, which took the tinge off any sadness I felt.

It was in a small eighties block and although the rooms were small, it was neat and tidy and they had everything they needed.

'It's alright ain't it, boys?' Jason smiled.

He put the pizzas in the oven while the boys showed me around.

He'd already set up their bedrooms and I knew it would start to look more cosy with more of their belongings in there.

Cooper and Keegan even had a bunk bed like they did at my house.

While the other two excitedly showed me round, Keegan was his usual reserved self.

Cooper and Billy went to watch TV in the living room while I helped Keegan put on the duvet cover we'd brought. I also put a little lamp on the floor next to the bottom bunk.

'There,' I smiled. 'It looks a lot cosier already.'

He suddenly had that familiar worried look on his face again.

My Brother's Secret

'It's going to be OK,' I told him, squeezing his hand.
'I know,' he nodded bravely.
Just then, Billy came running in.
'It's pizza time!' he shouted.

The rest of the evening passed quickly. After pizza on our knees in front of the telly, I knew I needed to leave them to it.

'Right, I'd better be off, boys,' I told them. 'Sleep well in your beds and remember Helen's going to be checking in with you in a few days.'

I gave Billy and Cooper a big hug. Then finally it was time to say goodbye to Keegan.

'You're going to be fine,' I told him quietly. 'But you know where I am if you need me.'

'Thank you,' he nodded. 'For everything.'

I swallowed the lump in my throat as Jason showed me out. At the door, he handed me a battered-looking box of Milk Tray, but it was the thought that counted.

'Thanks for everything you've done for my boys,' he told me. 'And I'm sorry, I really am.'

'I know you are,' I told him. 'But you're their dad and I can see you're trying.'

'Look after each other.'

As I walked back down the stairs and outside to my car, I clung on to the feeling of hope.

Despite what had happened in the past, I was impressed by the commitment Jason had shown to the boys and he'd done what he said and proved himself to Social Services. None of us knew what the future held, but he deserved that second chance to be their dad. I just hoped that, this time, it worked out.

Acknowledgements

Thank you to my children, Tess, Pete and Sam, who are such a big part of my fostering today. However, I had not met you when Amber, Cooper, Keegan and Billy came into my home.

To my wide circle of fostering friends – you know who you are! Your support and your laughter are valued.

To my friend Andrew B for your continued encouragement and care.

Thanks also to Heather Bishop who spent many hours listening and enabled this story to be told, my literary agent Rowan Lawton and to Anna Valentine, Vicky Eribo and Beth Eynon at Seven Dials for giving me the opportunity to share these stories.

Photo credit: Simon Way

Maggie Hartley has fostered more than 300 children while being a foster carer for over twenty years. Taking on the children other carers often can't cope with, Maggie helps children that are deemed 'unadoptable' because of their behaviour or the extreme trauma that they've been through.

She's looked after refugees, supported children through sexual abuse and violence court cases, cared for teenagers on remand and taught young mums how to parent their newborn babies.

You can find her on Facebook at MaggieHartleyAuthor, where she would love to hear from you.

What possesses a mum to kidnap her own child? That's what Maggie asks herself when she's asked to foster thirteen-year-old Saskia, the subject of a bitter custody battle between her parents. When Saskia's mum Rosa fears the courts are going to favour her ex-husband, James, she takes matters into her own hands.

With Rosa facing criminal charges, and Saskia refusing to live with her dad, her future looks uncertain. Will Maggie be able to step in and discover the bombshell that will tear this family apart?

Read on for an extract from *Don't Leave Me Here*, available now in paperback, ebook and audio

ONE

A Lost Cause

Thud.

Suddenly, my eyes flicked open and I sat up in bed.

What was that?

It was 11.30 p.m. and I'd only been in bed for half an hour. But sitting there in the darkness, the only thing I could hear was the sound of the blood rushing in my ears.

I must have been imagining it.

I lay back down and rested my head on the pillow. For the past week, I'd been living on adrenalin and seemed to be in a constant state of high alert.

I was currently fostering thirteen-year-old PJ. He was the only placement that I had at the moment, but he was a challenge to say the least.

He'd been in the care system since he was eleven, after his mum had left the area, abandoning him. Neighbours had found him starving and alone in his flat three days later, living off crisps and sweets he'd stolen from the local shop.

Over the past two years his behaviour had got worse as he was moved from one carer to another. Sadly, it was something I was seeing more and more frequently. He'd come to me after his current foster carers said they could no longer cope.

Never one to shy away from tricky placements, I'd said I'd take him in temporarily while a long-term solution was found.

For the first week or so, PJ had been fine. I wouldn't have called him chatty, but he had been OK, and he went to school and came straight home. Although he'd spent most of the time in his bedroom, we'd managed to have dinner together. I thought his previous foster carers must have been exaggerating about his behaviour. It was a few days later that I realised he had lulled me into a false sense of security. Things changed dramatically.

PJ had been skipping school and not coming home until late in the evening. When he did come back, he stank of weed. I'd noticed money had gone missing from my purse, so I'd started keeping my handbag locked away in my bedroom and updated his social worker and my supervising social worker about my suspicions.

This evening, he'd not come back after school until 10 p.m. – much too late for a thirteen-year-old.

'I won't tolerate this kind of behaviour in my house,' I'd told PJ when he'd finally turned up. 'As a foster carer, it's my responsibility to know where you are. So I need you to come straight home from school tomorrow. Do you understand?'

He'd shrugged, with his head down, and had spent the rest of the evening in his bedroom.

Before I'd gone to bed, I'd knocked on his door.

'What?' he'd grunted.

I'd pushed it open a chink.

'Night, PJ. Remember what I said about coming straight home tomorrow.'

'Yep,' he'd muttered.

It was a relief to see that he was already in his pyjamas and curled up in bed.

He was probably fast asleep by now and, if I could stop my mind playing tricks on me, I knew I needed to do the same.

I closed my eyes and tried to relax but I was still on hyper alert, listening out for any sound.

It's OK, I told myself. *You're imagining things.*

But sadly I wasn't.

Thud.

This time, there was no mistaking it. I jumped up out of bed and grabbed my dressing gown. PJ's bedroom door was closed but I could see the glow of a light coming from underneath it.

'PJ?' I asked, knocking on the door. 'Are you OK?'

No answer.

'I just want to check that you're OK in there.'

Silence.

'I'm coming in, I need to make sure you're OK.' I pushed open the door to find an empty bed and no sign of PJ.

'Oh no,' I gasped.

I bolted downstairs, as I realised that was where the noise must have been coming from. I ran into the kitchen first. I'd double-locked the front door and the patio doors and had put the keys in the kitchen drawer. Thankfully, they were still there. Then I dashed into the living room at the front of the house. Naively, I thought maybe he was in there watching TV.

But as I pushed open the door, a cold breeze hit me and told me everything I needed to know.

The lock on one of the bottom sash windows had been unscrewed. It was wide open, and PJ was gone. My bedroom was directly above the living room and I realised that the thud I'd heard must have been him opening the window.

With my heart racing, I unlocked the front door and ran out into the street. But it was too late. Even in the glow of the streetlights, I could see there was no sign of PJ. He had disappeared into the darkness.

It was always horrendous when a child went missing on your watch, particularly when it was a child you'd only been caring for for a few days.

I'd done it enough times over the years to know the drill by now.

First, I called the out-of-hours number at my agency and let them know that PJ had run off.

'I'll let Social Services know,' said Marion, the social worker on duty. 'If you could call the police, Maggie, and report him as missing and then ring me back with the crime number, that would be helpful.'

'Will do,' I said.

I knew the only issue with calling the police at this time of night was that they always took hours to come. A troubled thirteen-year-old who was in care sadly wasn't going to be at the top of the list of their priorities, especially one who had gone AWOL before. Once I'd reported PJ missing and got back to Social Services, I made myself a cup of tea to calm my nerves and settled onto the sofa.

I was shattered but I knew there was no point going back to bed, as there was a chance I wouldn't hear the door when the police arrived or if PJ came back. Besides, I was too worried and on edge to sleep. Over the years, I'd had several teenagers who had gone missing from time to time – in fact, there was one boy who ran off every couple of days. It was always concerning and stressful, but I knew all I could do was go through the proper processes and thankfully the police would always bring them back – or they'd eventually come back of their own accord. It was never a nice experience to go through, though.

It wasn't the most comfortable sofa, but it had acted as a makeshift bed for me many times over the years. As I tossed and turned, all I could think about was PJ. He thought he was tough and streetwise – but he was only thirteen and I knew that inside he was just a scared, vulnerable little boy who had been abandoned by his mother. My mind couldn't stop ticking over and over. *Where was he? Who was he with? What was he doing?*

I didn't sleep a wink and, just after 1 a.m., there was finally a knock at the door. I jumped up to answer it. Two female officers were standing on the doorstep. They held up their IDs and I showed them in.

'I'm PC Penny Brent and this is PC Helen Biller,' one of them said.

'I'm assuming that you need to search the house first?' I asked them.

They both nodded apologetically.

'You must have gone through this before?' asked PC Brent.

'Sadly, many times over the years with a variety of children,' I replied.

There was a protocol they had to follow when a child went missing and the first step was a thorough search of the house they had been in, just to check they weren't hiding somewhere. I knew of one foster carer who'd reported a child missing and it turned out they were hiding under their bed the whole time, so it could happen.

I'd done a quick check in every room myself and I was sure that PJ wasn't in the house, but I knew the officers had to check. I waited downstairs while they opened every cupboard, checked under every bed and even searched the shed in my back garden. I was relieved that I wasn't fostering any other children, otherwise they would have been disturbed by the search too.

As I'd expected, PJ was nowhere to be seen. Afterwards, I made us all a cup of tea while the officers took a statement from me.

'Has PJ done this before?' asked PC Biller.

'Not with me,' I said. 'He's been hours late after school but he's not gone missing this late before.'

'Do you have the names of any of his friends or know where he likes to hang out?' she added.

'Unfortunately, I don't know that much about him, as he's only just come to live with me.' I wrung my hands.

'You look worried,' said PC Brent.

'I *am* worried,' I replied. 'It's the middle of the night and he's only thirteen. He's missing and there's no guarantee that he's safe. People could be taking advantage of him. It's terrifying.'

'I can understand,' PC Brent nodded. 'We'll circulate his description to all of the local units and we'll do a drive round the local area and the town centre. Hopefully we'll have him back to you soon.'

'I hope so,' I said.

It was after 2 a.m. by the time the police left. I knew it was pointless trying to sleep now as I was wide awake and wanted to make sure that I heard PJ if he came back, as he didn't have a key. I decided to sit on the sofa and watch a film, desperately hoping I'd be disturbed by a tap on the window or a knock on the door.

By the time the film ended, there was still no sign of him. At some point during the second film, my eyes must have closed and I nodded off.

When I came round, daylight was streaming in through the living-room window. I looked at my watch. It was 8 a.m. and I could hear the hustle and bustle of the street outside as people headed off to work and school.

Maybe PJ was back and I hadn't woken up? I knew it was unlikely but I told myself perhaps he'd stolen a key and taken it with him, or forced his way in somehow? I rushed upstairs but my heart sank when I saw his empty bed.

It was at times like these that I was thankful I had no other children living with me at the time; I'd had a couple of respite placements that had lasted for a few months before PJ, as well as two longer-term placements. There was Amena, who I'd fostered for more than a year while her mum was in France caring for her aunt who was sadly dying of cancer. Then baby Felix, who I'd fostered for six months until he was able to be returned to live with his mum, Emily. Feeling like this, it would have been hard having to get up early and look after a baby or toddler, or even get another child to school.

I had a quick shower and got dressed but I was too tired and anxious to eat any breakfast. When it got to 9 a.m., I phoned my supervising social worker Becky as I knew she'd be starting work.

'Maggie, I've just read the update from the out-of-hours social worker,' she told me. 'Has PJ turned up yet?'

'No,' I sighed. 'Still no sign.'

'I'll give his social worker Carrie a ring and see if his former carers can think of anywhere he might have gone or who he might be with,' she told me.

'Good idea,' I agreed. 'It would be good to give the police that information.'

I also rang PJ's school and told them that he'd gone missing and wouldn't be coming in that day.

'Not for the first time,' sighed the receptionist.

By midday, nothing had changed. I hadn't heard anything from the police so I knew there couldn't be any update. To take my mind off things, I vacuumed the bedrooms, mopped the bathroom floor and dusted and tidied up everywhere. Cleaning was always my therapy when I was feeling stressed or anxious.

I was lugging the vacuum cleaner down the stairs when I heard a noise.

I stopped in my tracks as I heard a quiet knock on the front door.

Holding my breath, I opened it to find a dishevelled-looking PJ standing there.

'Thank goodness,' I sighed. 'I've been so worried about you. Where have you been?'

'Nowhere,' he scowled, pushing past me. He ran up the stairs and I heard his bedroom door slam.

I decided to let him cool off a bit before I tried to talk to him.

I called Becky first.

'He's just walked in,' I told her.

'What a relief!' she said. 'Where's he been?'

'Absolutely no idea,' I replied. 'He wouldn't talk to me.'

I told her what had happened and that he'd gone straight to his bedroom.

'I'll try to have a chat to him in a bit,' I said.

After I'd put the phone down, I called the police. PC Brent had given me her mobile number.

'PJ's just got back,' I told her.

'Oh, that is good news,' she replied. 'We'll come round.'

When a missing child returned, the police had to see them for themselves and talk with them about why they'd disappeared.

'We're going off shift soon so we'll head back round to you now,' she said.

'OK,' I nodded.

Two police officers turning up to talk to PJ might be exactly what he needed to realise that he couldn't behave like this.

Ten minutes later, I was just about to go up and check in with PJ as I knew the officers would be here soon, when suddenly he appeared in the kitchen doorway.

'You must be starving,' I said to him. 'Shall I make you something to eat?'

He looked at me and scowled.

'Who was you talking to?' he grunted. 'I heard you on the phone.'

'I was telling Social Services that you were back,' I told him. 'We were all really worried about you. The police were out looking for you too.'

I paused.

'They're going to come round now and have a chat with you about where you've been.'

'The police?' he shouted. 'Why the f*** did you call them? I don't wanna talk to the f***ing police!'

'PJ, you can't just go missing like that,' I told him. 'You're only thirteen.'

'I'll do what the f*** I want! I ain't taking orders from you!'

Suddenly there was a knock at the door and PJ froze.

'That will be the police now,' I told him. 'They just want to make sure you're safe.'

'I told you, I don't wanna talk to them,' he snarled. He glanced up at me. There was a rage in his eyes that made my blood run cold.

I tried to brush past him to let them in but as I did, he grabbed my arm. Even though he was only thirteen, he was already taller than me and his grip was strong.

'Don't answer the door,' he hissed.

Before I knew what was happening, he pushed me to the floor. Then he lifted one of the kitchen dining chairs up in the air.

'PJ, no!' I shouted, instinctively holding my arms up to protect my face.

But it was too late. He threw the wooden chair and it hit me directly on the head.

My body trembled in shock and my head throbbed. I blinked as I felt something dripping into my right eye. As I raised my hand up to it, I realised that it was blood.

PJ looked terrified. He saw the blood and turned around and ran out of the kitchen. I struggled to my feet to try to follow him.

He pulled open the front door and ran outside where PC Brent and PC Biller were waiting on the front path.

'Hey!' they shouted as he tried to push past them. PC Brent managed to grab his arm.

I stumbled to the doorway and they both gasped.

'What on earth has been happening here?' asked PC Brent.

PJ struggled and tried to get out of her grip.

'Penny, do you want to take him to the car while I sort Maggie out?' said PC Biller.

I could see PJ was still struggling as PC Brent led him down the path.

'It's OK,' PC Biller nodded to me. 'She'll wait with him in the car while he calms down.'

I was still in shock as she led me to the sofa and sat me down.

'Let me get something for that head of yours,' she told me.

My head was throbbing and suddenly I felt very woozy.

'Could I have a glass of water, please?' I mumbled.

PC Biller fetched me a drink and some kitchen roll to press against my head to try to stem the bleeding. She sat with me while I had a few sips of water and took some deep breaths and, gradually, my heart rate started to slow down.

'So can you tell me what happened?' she asked.

I described how PJ had returned to my house and then come downstairs.

'He said he didn't want to talk to the police and when you knocked on the door, he pushed me over and threw a kitchen chair at me.'

'Gosh,' PC Biller sighed. 'That cut on your head looks small but deep. I think you need to go to the hospital and get someone to have a look at it, as you might need stitches.'

'Really?' I said. 'Surely it's not that bad?'

'Really,' she nodded.

'But what about PJ?' I asked.

'What he did is assault,' she told me. 'So he's going to be coming back to the station with us as we need to ask him a few questions. Do you have the number of his social worker, please?'

I nodded. PC Biller passed me my handbag from the side of the sofa. I got out my mobile and gave her Carrie's number.

'We would have given you a lift to the hospital, but obviously we've got PJ in the car,' she said apologetically.

'It's fine,' I said. 'I'll get a taxi to A&E.'

'Is there anyone I can call to come with you?' she asked. 'A partner?'

'No, it's just me,' I smiled. 'I'll be fine.'

'Well, I'll ring a cab for you and stay with you until it arrives,' she told me. 'We don't want you collapsing.'

Thankfully the taxi arrived in ten minutes.

I still felt quite wobbly and my forehead was throbbing, so I was glad that PC Biller helped me lock up the house. As I walked down the path, I saw PJ in the back seat of the police car with PC Brent.

He scowled at me and looked away.

I felt upset and annoyed at myself. I think, deep down, I had naively and stupidly thought I was the one who could make a difference to him and turn his behaviour around.

But I'd been wrong.